The Calliope Waltz

Edward Wolverton

PublishAmerica
Baltimore

PublishAmerica has allowed this work to remain exactly as the author intended, verbatim, without editorial input.

ISBN: 978-1-61546-231-5
PUBLISHED BY PUBLISHAMERICA, LLLP
www.publishamerica.com
Baltimore

Printed in the United States of America

To Marie,
To whom I would love
To Share This Wonderful Dance

Edward Wolverton
10/25/11

Table of Contents

Chapter 1

1.
Something to Say—Something to Forget

Out of life
We gather nuts for winter's gale,
As life shines the sun
Shall our seeds fall to become trees.

I feel the day
That tomorrow is gone,
And yesterday
We have played all day long,
Waited my minute's sorrow
Tasted my joys of life.

I feel the heavy burden
That life sings upon the trees,
With the breath of yesterday
The tears fall the distance of life,
Befalls my throne to love.

I have something to say
That I ever regret,
I never forget,
The set passages of life,
From childhood
To become a man,
For to say
That love does not matter
Would be,
My eyes—too blind to see.

Something to be said about love
And the temptress abides
Sweeping my soul
Into the bonds of holy morrow.
My most sound shall speak,
Is the wonder of my love to seek,
But that
It has to be said.

A winter's past
And the shells hidden away,
As the trees have shed their fruit
All I ask of myself
Is to love—but truth,
As I gather there
The fruits there of.

2.
Way of Forest Golden Sun

Raindrops of light
Giving life to color,
And golden sun to rise
And shine my forest…

The cool brisk air
That flows a mountain stairway,
falls from the skies of blue
And water too…
Touching velvet skirts of golden sun,
To run fingers through my hair
And casting shadows of glitter-silver
Sliding the rails of river foam,
To become mist of my eyes
By way of forest golden sun.

I look into the forest trees
Golden from the searching sun,
And fields of river wood
Splashing into the sky.
As treasures hold,
And fall from mountain's side,
As river's reach to grab the gold
And tuck it deeply under safety locks,
Slipping under deep river rocks,
And trees to drink, and glitter
From the taste of eve,
A way of forest golden sun.

The winding wind to curve
And curb just above the trees,
As water melts a standing rock
Into a many pebbled sea,
And glitters silver sky.
Lying upon the water's crest,
Slowly slipping from the miles,
To lay wind upon the sea of rock,
And golden sun sits above the trees.
Shining golden runs from out the earth,
Hold quartz of white, and diamond's glare
A layer of melting sun, to rock of ages be,
By way of forest golden sun.

3.
A Communion with Life and Soul

Dare we speak of a communion
That does share with life and love,
That a soul should be-,
Ever be set aside.

Enter
The mixture of life,
Where upon a doorway
Has opened,
To bring upon us
A love so divine.

The exaltation of granted wishes
Shall storm the doors of life,
And become the dreams of man
And choose his destiny.
A communion with the soul
To re-enact his birth,
Till death has no more visions to see.

Grace shall abide
And the soul shall survive,
With hopes and wishes of love,
Coming fast at the door
That opens wide.
My heart to become the swift passion,
And my eyes to see this love,
And take Holy communion,
That my soul shall forever live.

To be
What life has thrown upon us,
Yet the wisdom to be this love,
And conquer all of life
In dormant values of the mind.
To wake…
Is to see this great love,
And life shall follow us through,
Into a new beginning with time
As the communion.

It is to swear upon us
The most sacred thoughts
Of life, and love,
And in remembrance to this oath,
Shall we forever see the light
Of all that is,
And all that shall forever be.

To kiss the soul
With life,
That love shall forever keep
Within the heart,
And the soul…
Weak or strong,
Shall be touching
Living life,
And love will spill
Of ages past,
To fill the cup of time.

We now have communion
With the Holy,
Of ourselves.

4.
The Wind Will Blow

The wind will carry
What weeping words I own,
To the secrets of the city
And into the hills of all concrete,
Past the trees of sobriety.

Soul sounds the city
Where wind pipes a weary pity,
Whipping to a child
Crying in the wind,
And woe to the mild
Of hunger pains.

I see there
Lying in the darkness,
Staring into an alleyway,
A soul that has given up hope.
Forever living in the shadows of discontent,
To die from the cold.

The fever is a bottle,
The most of it.
Whispering into the ears of a friend,
Sharing what they spent.

The darkness hides
The luminary friend,
Shouting out in blinking language,

Saying come on in…
Your welcome here,
As long as your dollar
Floats the table.

The strippers gaze at the doorway
Hoping to produce a john for later on,
And ave' mercy on him…
The soul,
That was suckered in.

The darkness holds
What the wind will blow
Into all directions,
And the secrets spill
From out the night.
Hoping for just a little jubilation,
But presses onward
Into the soul's lament.

A thief
Wanting to take your money.
Hand over the wallet
And no one gets hurt,
As he shoots him anyway,
Just to watch him die.

The prince of the city
All pimped up and ready,
To take his girls out for a ride.
Take them in stride,
And pull out the money
From their cheaper tricks.

The police,
Lights flashing,
Radio blasting,
Find a body
Hidden behind a dumpster,
And report it in.
To send out a message to the collector
And the chief inspector,
Waiting for the county coroner.
Maybe to see him
Three or four hours later,
To pronounce that the soul is dead,
And shovel the body off to the morgue.

The tall giants echo the streets
With gunfire and sirens.
The loop of flashing red lights
On every corner,
Asking a friend
For a dime in the hand.

The lights
A little brighter now,
With the needle sticking in,
And pumping the force of the wind
Into his veins.
Cries out,
Craps out,
Into a rough ride.
A small bit of rat poison,
And another soul dies.

The wind will blow
Where secrets keep well into the shadows,
Where darkness sleeps

To whisper deep strange bed fellows.
To whisper into the ears
May call some of those to awake,
As a city lays wait
Innocent of all dying things.

5.
Dying.
Into Silence

For Virginia [2007]

What words are life,
When the wind whispers away
The voice of reason ?

The tears are for you.

We grieve the silent tears
For yesterday,
For today is a new beginning.

We cry when storms arise
My friend,
Fare thee well
Of silent days ahead.

Oh' sweet pedestal of life
To have given sacrifice,
My honored friend.
Not a breath or a will to speak
For the flowers wilt with time.

Into silence,
Souls may be dead,
To seal thy fate,
And the poet sings of a passing truths.

Where once we were friends,
And I can remember you.

So shared for sorrow
The many memories,
Of now, thy silent sleep.
Weep for me,
As I weep for you,
For now you lay upon
The winds of time,
And still
We weep for you.

6.
I Hand My Heart

I hand my heart
For he who weeps with me,
The silence of my many years.

I weigh upon the judgment of honor
My thoughts upon a Libra scale,
To feel the freedom that I have once lived
My heart that forever feels.

I hold upon my hand held heart
As a gift to the glory of the sky,
As a show to the greatness of my love
Outnumbered upon my finger's scrolls.

I hold my heart
And hand it freely upon the winds of love,
Reaching for the light well into the day
The miles before I run.

I am the towering light house
That fills the sky with light,
From the coastal running sands
I greet the hour glass of time.

I am the mighty cypress
Who holds firm the cliff's of tide,
Leaning to an onshore breeze to a flow of air
A breath that I bestow.

I look into a sea of time
As the waves of life beat upon the rocks,
My heart sounds the trumpet of the fog
The cold gray of a shinning sun.

May be this my beating heart
Slowly sifting sand from the sea shore,
To love the elements of the sea
The sand, the wind, the rocks, the shore.

I hand my heart
To Weigh upon the sea of life,
Or sail the love of burning eyes,
To the sky I hold a beating heart.

7.
Projection of a Higher Light

In the time of life
A pin drops,
To listen
One can hear the cries
Of earth.
The light upon my soul
Bleeds the laughter of the wind,
The light that shines upon me
Will be my life in content.

I hear the organ grinder
This wave of sound hits my ears,
I see the monkey running
To catch a penny in the air.

I feel the blind man's justice
As he holds a pencil in a cup,
Listening for a coin to drop
And never miss a cent.

It must be God
That shines upon the street,
And holds the hidden sights of day
As though we could not speak.

The rubble of all mankind facing
As I hear the organ grinder pacing,
And the monkey chasing pitiful dimes
As the blind man smiles to the music.

It must be God
Who shows me the higher light,
A genesis of light
That soothes the soul into peace.

There must be a light
That shines before my very soul,
As the city lights begin to fade away
And life falls back to sleep again.

I hear the organ grinder
Walking down the street,
Captivating all
Into a sea of sound.
In the middle of a cement city
Down towards east of main,
I hear the footsteps tattered feet
Pounding leathered souls.
Engraving the pencil mark upon the street,
A society of high light and color,
That turns stop lights yellow on a street,
And people stop on a corner never to meet.

The wave of sound hits my ears
As the shining light hits my eyes,
This life that dreams in many colors,
This life that hears of many sounds,
Alive, and waiting to live.
Waiting to move
When the light turns green again.

The light that glows a neon white
As every sign in the city is turning on,
As the cement and glass mixes to reflect of the sun
And seeing the emerald lights of Broadway.

Counting steps before the next corner crossing
And the people gather on a street corner again,
In a maze of a cement jungle,
At a loss for words
In the distance of time.

To travel to a place called nowhere
Where souls must gather,
And be aware of each other
As a change of light,
Starts the motion of walking again.
Where the blind are leading the blind,
And nowhere leads to everywhere,
We all want to go.

As I hold myself into the light
And listen to the organ grinder,
And watch for his monkey jumping the lights,
And the blind man listening to footsteps,
And coins landing in his tin cup.

It must be God
For all intent and praise,
Who has shown me this sight to see.
A new found day into my heart,
And all the rubble of mankind,
And the light turning red.

Chapter 2

8.
Dreams to Remember Me By

Such is life,
That we dream away
The hours of time.
Such is love,
That the dreams
Will always come.
Such is a dream,
That lives
in the memories of us all.

Dream my soul
Into your thoughts,
Is what my heart desires.
To live in your thoughts
As a dream that becomes
A wish to the heart,
So seems my will of thoughts
That you shall forever be.

A dream,
In a time of life
Where love once roamed,
Shall seek the times remembered.
As those that are alone
I shall forever keep,
And shall dream of you.

The keeper of the flame
In the name of love,

Where the truth does dare
Or share such dreams,
Shall be my heart
That death not know,
Will be upon the sight
Of a dream that I will follow.

What dreams
My love came to be,
To see you in my dreams
And feel you in my heart,
That love and life
Are much the same,
And flows my soul
Into the bosom of the wind,
To touch you so.

The night brings to me
Such love,
To feel upon my soul
Your sweet touch,
And your dreams
To grab upon my search,
And want me so.

The wishful wind
To passage by our love,
Renews the vows taken
Even after death.
Shall we speak the dreams
Of eternity,
To rise within myself,
And the long lonely night.
Shall prevail the winds tonight,
For you
To be with me.

A dream of lost time
When memories were forgotten,
Comes calling into the wind
Flowing upon my breath
To speak to you,
And I will the way
With love to remember,
As a dream I have of you
That mute sounds will surrender.

My heart is a dream
As my love for you encounters,
Such life upon the wind of morrow,
Fades into the shade of a tree.
Upon our carved names
Into the wooded bark,
And sweet our memories shall be known,
That you dream of me.

A chance to feel the dreams
What night ponders,
Past the soul
To flow into the heart,
And wander upon the night
Till the dream encounters,
This feeling we share.
To come into the night as a whisper,
And save my sanity with your love.

To chance a dream
And surrender the night upon the wind,
As a whisper my many thoughts to you.
As you sleep and dream,
My will to send to you my love
Upon the many lonely nights,

That I cannot be with.
Shall keep in secrets our love
That moves the night away,
And the dreams will encounter
Us together,
Just one more time.

9.
Endearment of Heart

Praise the folly of a man in love
To raise the love that will be,
Such endearments spilling from his heart
To come…to come…
To be.

The quiet of me
Calls upon the spirit of my soul,
Such love is my heart
That roses bloom the fields,
And poppies burn the sky.

I reach towards the eyes of God
Holding upon the beaten path,
The sojourner of truth to become my guide
As I hide away my eyes from the sorrow of the day,
And field my visions of tomorrow.

I wake my soul
To seek the slender tree of life,
Watching the stems widening my path
As it shields the forest floor from pain,
As I refrain the thoughts
And touch sweet love,
My heart's endearment.

I whisper the faint of heart
This joys that touches my soul,
And bleed the stems of roses dare

To care for one another,
As this path shall seal our fate.

I will stream the visions of my eyes
To sleep the heart in slumber's passion,
Regret to the soul to touch my friend
I find myself another,
And become what fate would call my name
In the touch of my endearments.

I will touch,
And feel the love obey
What commands my soul to scream,
And reach for the pleasant of such memories
Within my touch,
To grasp at things that roam my mind,
Upon a long endearment of time.

I will hold of thought
Looking unto a silver moon turn blue,
Chase the memories of thought
To become of what friends shall be,
As I touch the endearment of your soul,
In such a time of need.

My words floating upon the wind
And time unravels the hemp rope of my heart,
From holding you close to me,
And my endearment with love
Shall keep the many memories of ourselves,
Contemplating to the paths of life.

I step into the stock raving mind of a man
Blinded by the search of love,
Finding my true soul mate friend I love
Holding onto my soul for life,
As we sail the seven seas
Enduring endearing times.

10.
The Composition of a Life-Long Dream

The composure of my thoughts
Begin,
In early morning sunshine.

We dream the inadequate
Of a day long song.
We rise to see the sun
Burst into rays of golden bride,
Where once there was darkness,
But now contrite light
Upon the wings of heaven.
Our sight blending colors,
Blending bleeding tones of life.

I feel fortunate
That I am alive.
For death…
Has knocked upon my door,
And I had hidden in the darkness of my fear.
Hidden there
Where my soul was bare,
And I could not live
Without my heart pounding there,
And it was stopped.

My dreams, elusive,
Fallen into the pits of time.
My wants
Gathered into the nothingness,

And poured upon my soul
Like gallons of shivering water.
As a galore of dreams,
Frozen.
Now wanting to commit
To the bareness of time,
And seek out the nakedness of life,
As the old one
Has fallen away.

A composition of my dreams
To fulfill all my fantasies.
A bright or morning star,
To gather round my soul
And beg me forgiveness,
That I could not answer
A simple doorbell,
When it was time to awaken my eyes,
Because death was so near.
As death has interrupted
The sleep of my very eyes,
Why death is so dark and dreary
That I cannot ever begin to sleep again.

The illusions of life
Taken away,
But the dreams persist,
And my heart begins to beat again,
As I open my eyes to life,
And my heart is beating again.
My heart,
Truly in want of life,
Succumbed to do battle with death,
But waits upon the rise of the sun,
And is reborn
Into the dreams that are yet to become.

11.
A Flower of Wishful Love

The flower of a sunlight rose pedal
Sweeps the beautiful rise,
My checkered stars for eyes
To cry the beauty of love.

Sweet song
The call of love.
To shine upon the window's maze,
For flowers bloom in sunshine splendor
About the window box,
Where it is of my heart that lays.

In silence
Softly spoken truths.
My heart races from the act of love,
Sweet charms and kisses form
My lips,
To whisper sweet a melody as love,
And sing upon the gentle winds
My heart to pound.

A flower,
To become my mate.
A sweet soul
That gathers upon my eyes,
This love to gratify my wait
In wanting lure,
So gently stirs my heart to pound
In the sounds of wind to whisper love.

I wish,
Upon a flower field,
That love will burst
And shine my eyes.
So sweet a smell as a scent of a rose
To choose my heart to pound with love.
I beg and plead for my thoughts,
For a flower of wishful love.

12.
Whispers of a Child

I thought I was
To be,
The one who listened well,
But find myself listening to nothing.
No more,
Until I opened my eyes
And saw it was the whimper,
A voice of a child,
Who has cried many tears.

My dry eyes to fear
What a voice might hear,
Be spoken for the words
Of a child.
I hear what voice begins
Whimpering in the wind.
To cry upon this child,
That sends what love
I know.

My eyes would focus well,
But my mind wanders.
In the dust of the wind,
It wonders in the lust of life.
This child would keep to my heart,
Speak to my soul.
To speak and cry with me,
If only for a little while.

I would feel the tears multiply
And my thoughts would take a chance
To look at the child,
Listen to the child,
And I would feel my inner heart whisper
To the child,
Who cried intensely upon my ears,
To comply my love to heart.

The whispers of a child
Who would keep my heart,
And speak to me,
Before anyone's sake.
As I implore my heart to goodness,
And rake the tears away,
And hold the child so dear to my soul,
So close to my own heart.

13.
To Whom the Poet

To whom the poet
Of whom I speak,
The words of my tomorrows
Wander upon my feet,
The greatness that will never stop,
Speaks for us all.

I travel the winds of ultimate time
And from the words of yesterday,
I am done and fade away,
What verse or prayer I say,
Unless a poet
Who becomes so real,
To feel the power of his words.

I listened to the wind prevail
What voice I would sail into time,
What words would I see
And those that were blind,
His vise was a voice of words,
The tears of atonement was his choice,
The words fell from his heart.

To whom the poet doth speak
For friend and foe alike,
In any given time.
To honor what words rivers flow
Will cost the tears on a lakeshore's edge,
And swallow the winds from yesterdays past,
As time passes before our very eyes.

To whom my heart poured out
To whom the poet will speak,
The Winter's edge must come to meet
And the Summer sails what floats to retreat,
And shall the storms of life arise,
As the sun will speak of destiny
At my feet,
The poet speaks of all my years.

14.
Little Blessings

Cry out
Little child,
Little woe, and want for love.

Cry my little ones,
For fear and dread and stone
Who knows me not,
But that I know
You were left alone.

Little child
My child,
Where little blessings stood.
Upon the years of time
I will forever hear your cries,
If ever anybody would.

You are my child
Left in the house of time,
And I have lost your sweet smile
With such little blessings.
This love that once such bright eyes,
From the emptiness of your fate,
That I could not take you away.

My time,
My father's time,
When you were the sought seeds of love
That brought my heart to live.

These years from us
Taken apart,
Would mend a broken heart,
And see the blessings
That you are.

Dear child,
Sweet smile upon your dirty face,
Who grins at the master of time and place.
Who will seal your fate
That you know me not,
And I would see you grow
From the child you once were.

Chapter 3

15.
Ghost Passion

I swear
I never meant to write this,
But something was aging me on…
So I will tell the tale-
Where words will swallow.

Stitch the touch of time
Oh' weary one,
It is I,
The ghost of love and passion,
Here to greet you at the door of death.

Never have I said,
That love would fall upon your shadow,
But wake upon the bed of death.
Dire so near,
And to touch this morbid love upon my lips.

I grasp at life,
And gasp for love.
That love would have no more emotions for me
Except to die a long and lonely death,
With a love to follow me to the grave.
Oh, I concede this fact of fate,
To give away my own true ghost.

I wish for love
To remain on the life side,
Begging for hope in another world

Where passions will not visit.
That now I can feel this pain of want,
Even after death.

I say this,
Because
Love is so full of life
That it might do me harm to ingest.
I have reason to resist,
For my love is lost in vain of thoughts,
Forever to become as my mortal sin.

Ghost passions
Of the nighttime bliss,
Go do me no harm
And fill my wants elsewhere.
For I have surrendered my soul
Upon passion's bed,
As death has touched my lips,
And turned me gray ground old.

I roam the night
So sore displeased,
But want not of the favored things in life,
For death has done me wrong.
I resist the temptations of life
Because of this,
That I am gone forever now.
Just a ghost in hollowed need,
That once prayed for love.

16.
The Children of Zoel

There is a place under the two suns,
Where the orange lit sky turns blue.
In the dark of evening brisk,
And the children played contently
Without a worry in the world,
It is these children of Zoel
Who have magic in their souls.

I swipe the sky
Reaching my arms to length
Of a child,
And touch my own dreams.
Falling into my own mind
From the clouds of cotton haze,
These children seem to give
Magic upon their thoughts,
That I dream of so many colors
Within the smiles of their eyes.
My mind can barely think
My own words.

This be child of Zoel
Who cast spells and plots,
To dream our souls
In chance.
We are the wise ones,
But the child will make an advance
And store the words within a wish,
To have you bound tightly with the light of day.

Upon the kiss
Of magic in their eyes.

The suns rise East and West
To pass the sky each way,
Touching shadows of each they turn
Into the eyes of a child.
Glowing red the sounds of sight,
To bleed my ears of thought,
That a child could say
The wonders of the Universe,
With one touch of a finger
Upon your forehead.

This child of Zoel
Holds out the hands of miracles,
To shade into the space of the suns.
Where the orange sky meets
Upon the blue of night,
And crests the bowl of fifteen moons.
To shine the stars of magic dust
Into my eyes,
And I realize that the apple upon the tree
That Eve picked,
Was for me.
Adam stood watching,
As I bit the battles of sin.

My now wisdom
Was faint,
A low hearted blow upon my brow,
As I sweated tears of fear and death.
As new life entered my veins,
As I fought upon my very soul
And I could see the vast forever,
The stars that shine upon time.

Fate stood staring into my eyes,
As so did this child,
Who beaconed with bright eyes,
Burning light into my soul.

This child of Zoel
Became lost of me,
That I had taken part of this magic
And swarmed the sight of the two suns.
I gathered the moons to rise
Upon the North of winds,
That I could whisper words
Into the ears of babes,
And they would listen to me,
With open eyes.

I felt the sweet touch
Of anger and mood,
But began to feel the ease of love
That these children I knew.
I was their father,
I was their mother,
And only I could love them
As a child would ever know.
In passing before the words were thought,
We would touch sight of this,
That the suns became as one,
And united our souls together.
The moons fell as one,
To become the master
Of our own words,
That we would speak
Upon the many days with each other.

This
Was understood,

And we had no way of knowing further
Of what magic might occur between us,
But we entered into the circle of love,
And pain had fell away.
These clouds burst into tears of joy,
Where man and child could grow together
In the balmy white of their eyes.
To hide the secrets of magic within there souls,
And hold each other in arms of lost beasts,
And reach for the goodness in life.

It is understood
That the children of Zoel
Became the caretakers of the Universe.
But without the love of a man,
They were only dark shadows of fear,
Swept dust,
Under a carpet of living planets.
As now the whispers of thought
To be created between man and child,
Was the love that they both shared,
And the magic of life, reborn,
Giving way to a new life,
A new Universe,
A voice of love.

17.
On the Eve of My Destruction

War torn,
That peace was known
For men and honor,
Do we raise upon ourselves
That life and death
Are much the same,
And to become as one?

Bitter enemies,
Me, myself, and I.
To have fallen from my state upon life,
My state of grace to fade away,
To see death in an un-natural way.

I hope to fall asleep someday
And never be asked to wake up.
For the pain of death
Is so sharp unto my heart,
Unto my breasts,
And I can resist,
What passions do I implore?

I have dignity
And reason within my own self,
And raise no suggestions that any man may
See me die in disgrace,
For the pain of it all
Would surely make me cry.

On the eve of my destruction,
I shall pray heed, deeply upon the words of God.
Hoping for justification in my own life,
And redemption to my soul that I would so surely need,
To become immortal in the words of time.

It is I
Who hesitates death,
As life is so strong in need,
And I cannot reason with myself
To go any further into death.
For what grasps at my time of need,
I shall surely live.
What say I
That death has no hesitation,
That death has no institution.
For the many are weary worn,
And have given proper proclamation,
And have reason to deal with death,
That I not go
For when I am called,
As the door of death opens wide
To take me asunder.

What thunder doth' roar
That death be not proud,
That I seek the words of death
And I see the tears of life,
Linger upon my years.
I sing the songs of moral dignity,
And raise the hand to orchestrate the masses
Into the music of life.
Given death has no rewards,
But to keep sake and sanity safe,
As we flake into the pits of dust.

On the eve,
That I shall fall to my knees
And plead for my very own soul,
I will question why life has given me up,
And maybe protest once too much,
For I am not ready for death,
And maybe never will be.
But to live forever,
Is truly out of the question,
And I must relinquish life
At its bounds.

On the eve of death,
I shall fear not.
For I have reasoned with myself these facts,
And have taken into new sights of passage,
And go with the blessings of God.

18.
The Hollow of My Eyes

It is the hollow of my hand
That bleeds my memories,
To make me blind.
It is the hollow of my heart
That makes me cry
For sexual desires.
I pray to touch,
The grand scale of entrance.

I comb the bits of hair about my head
Flying in the wind a glider that looms,
To seek my fair heart in splendor's fair.
As I wash my hands,
And will my way into my finder's say,
Blowing a wish,
Or dare a kiss.

The hollow of my eyes
To fill my heart with love,
That I grasp ascension of.
A holy mass in union
To a maker's peace of mind,
I would give my birth
To a new found lease,
And care upon the wine of time,
My juice,
My justice shall prevail.

The hollow of my eyes could see
The dampness in my life
From the tears of verse,
My cost to the sea of time
Where once I was blind.
Now knows where love comes from,
And I hold the keys to love,
Only to open the deep of my heart
To spill the open door of tears into my eyes.

I hold the hollowed love
Within the hollow of my hands,
To bare witness to my thoughts in nakedness.
This witness into my soul
Falling into the melting sand,
That love could exist
Within the right frame of mind,
And hold true to mine…
What thoughts would dare
And flare into the wind.
The shadows of my care
Would speak to me.

To touch the emerald sea with love
I would obey my sins to trust,
And feel the warmth of my breath
Sweet lure of heart,
Become my nakedness to this day
And open wide my soul to pray.
Into new oblivions that I would share
And fall into the pits of hell,
To obey my wanting sins.

I will hold the secrets of love
And touch your heart to dare,
Such a sweet heart to share,
And with what roaming finger's touch
Sweet smell of youth.
My fires to clutch an open flame
What one thought of you I could see,
And open flame would flicker for me
From the hollow of my eyes.

19.
Whimpers of an Only Child

I thought I would be
The one who cried well,
As I could find myself listening
To the tears of a child.
Until I opened my heart
And cried many tears,
For I was this child.

My dry eyes ached
And fell into fear,
What spoken voice was heard
But the cry of a child in need.

My eyes could only focus
Upon the smiles of tomorrow,
But my mind would wander
As I wondered where I came from,
Or who this child would be.
This, and that, or the other things,
As I could hear my inner tears comply
With what voice of the wind I heard,
My thoughts would find in my verse
And cry the many things of my heart.

The whispers of a child
Would speak to me-
As age became my sake,
And I fell ill in a gray flannel suit.
Holding for proper attire

To stance upon the wind,
And cry as this child in vain.
What tears were given at my birth upon this day,
As I held out my hands
To catch the sweet whimpers of life.

I fear myself to run away,
With what voice I would shout
Upon the whispers of my despair.
As a child I would cry the many tears,
Holding my hands upon the heart
And ask him to bless me so,
Knowing that I could not fall away
From this thing a child would call love.
That things would be alright
As the eyes were open tight,
To love upon this finger hold.

20.
Moments of Life

Sobriety conforms to humanity
The wishful thoughts of society.
Take care, and may God bless
The sweet moments of life
That which are so dear,
That I can remember
Upon this day.

I remember
To awaken,
To say at my birth,
As to which such moments
Are so dear to me.
I will not forget,
Nor will I choose to deceive myself
When gray matters are getting me old,
But to live by order and grace,
That all such things will pass away.

Life is spoken for,
As is lived for
On a daily basis.
To whom the rewards are given
By the grace of them being awake,
Shall keep thought of this
In remembrance of fair shadows.
To keep well my days upon foot,
For so soon are we to become
Of what dust enacted us.

So soon
We will tell
In just notification,
As how we see the world
Within our own eyes.
As how we are to declare upon it,
And grasp upon its contents
Whole heartedly.
Speaking of virtually anything that moves
Or to be put upon us at any given hour
In our time of need, to do within our lives,
As we so
Deem fit.

21.
Loving Eyes

To the child who is homeless
Please worthy praise.
The eyes that are aimless
Shall speak for the many souls,
For the world is at our doorstep
And good grace is in our hearts.

The heart of a child
Who cries upon the night
For want of a love that so binds,
This child of worthy eyes
Who has no name,
Shall speak to me in dreams
Looking from the eyes of the world.

The child knows of love
But cannot understand of its concept,
For fear of lost reprisal,
That life has once taken it away.
Sweet cries of this child
With loving eyes,
Who cries distant in the world of wind,
Only knows the truth of life
And where it is for the moment.

This homeless child strays
that shames the world,
To feel so alone
And wishes for care.

I begin to question my own sanity
As I wish for the child
Of such sweet a forgotten memory.
These forgotten songs of earth,
To please come home to me.

The orphaned child
That sings upon the night,
Of holy cries to birth.
Sweet love and tenderness my child
Who speaks with silent woes and tears,
To find what love it knows.
The child who smiles into the face of life,
Now looking
Into the eyes of love,
Holds my hand in the face of Good cheer,
And such sweet graces of God.

Chapter 4

22.
A Red Palmed Rose with a White Peace Dove

Dear peace,
Give me sweet joy today.

I hold the rose,
Who's blood turns red
As war,
Once fed the memories
That now become blind.
I turn my head,
That my eyes may not see
That death is eternal.

My hands bleed,
As I see this nightmare
Arise upon my eyes.
For when I sleep,
And now it stays
In daytime wait,
Where I become
immune to it.

Joy,
That peace may hold
A white dove,
To fly into the skies,
And my eyes see
Life eternal.

Death,
Shall hold me free no more.
That what life falls from us,
We shall lose forever.

Touch the faded rose
That bleeds,
And see the soft born skin
Fade away into memory.

To hold the bird of peace,
We shall hear peaceful moments with God,
And praise all eternal sight,
That war is no more.

All things will pass
And we are still asking ourselves,
Who to kill,
Friend or foe.

I say
To hold the bird of white pearl,
And raise it in your arms,
Lifting it high into the heavens,
That you shall become pure of heart.

I say
What love shall see,
That the rose will bleed
As war must pass,
Or thorns may grow
Upon the vines of life,
And bleed much upon your soul.

I hold the white dove.
Isn't it enough,
To show what peace is
That I ask for?

I hold
The red blooded rose
That cries the tears of man.
Sweet of rose,
That I should kiss you.

I stand here bleeding,
Looking into the wind of time,
And search for peace,
Where ever it might be.

I stand alone bleeding
Looking from a soul as one,
To pray heed of war,
And hold the white bird
In my hands.
To hold the white dove
With mercy in my eyes,
And beg for peace
For until the morrow.

United,
We shall carry the dove
To new highs,
And hold the red rose of life,
That God shall see.
The snows of white flake calm
to touch the lips of man,
And kiss his soul…
And cry peace
As this eternal love.

23.
Once to Be the Light of My Being

Forever,
I shall see the stars
To fall gracefully from yesterday.
As enthused shall be my morrow,
To entertain my eyes
Upon this day.

I offer
A free hand and heart,
To be the light of my being.
It is a choice matter
To believe in one's self,
And not hide
In the shadows of life.

The serene sun
Grows to perfection,
The heat of my heart
And the shine of my soul,
Into a vast universe of life
In my time of day.

I have omitted nothing
As the life of me.
The light of my being,
Comes from
The glory of God.

I shall shine into the vast of my void,
Into the light of infinity.
My soul lives and shines,
That may live on forever,
And my heart shall beat
The whispers of silent stars,
To shine upon a night lit sky.

I shall become as one
With the universe.
Granting life long dreams
And enchanting verse,
To muse my soul.

My eyes bright with the full moon
Will give such sweet love,
As fate comes near to love another.
As my heart is like a tree-
It bends and bows with
The wind of time.
To retreat, and send
Such love,
As the bright of my eyes
Soon shall see
To convey my inner thoughts.

I float aimlessly upon the stars
To grant light upon the night,
And hold love upon the earth.
As the seas shall bring life,
From the gathering of waves.
As God becomes
My light,
And the light of my being.

24.
Kindness to a Soul

My life,
For fear the end of it,
Has gracefully fallen tears
Of joy and hope,
That within my life
Love will come,
And show me how to live.

I feel wonder
And see serene images,
Not to wish of talking
Dirty laundry,
But to cleanse the dirt
From my soul.

It is I
Who wanders the wind
To say goodbye,
Once seeking fame and fortune,
And now ending up
In the gutter of truth.
Oh, that my soul
Shall see,
The grit of it.

Warm hands, cold of heart,
My soul to be
Heated hands
With a warm heart.

That will forgive
The coldness of life,
And choose for me,
One to love.

What must I do,
To prove my worthiness
Of your sweet friendship?
I slowly kill myself from
The hate of the world,
As well the lust upon it,
This age of my salvation.

My book of life
Forever upon the wheel of mankind,
Has its own revelations,
Its own self worth.
To be truthful
Unto one's self
And a kindness to others,
Begging forgiveness
For the sins of time.

I am a just, and rightful person,
Searching for
The kindness of a soul.
So suffers my friends
To be as little children,
The worthiness of my distractions.
To mend a broken heart,
And have mercy
Upon love's lost world.
To suffer my kindness,
My love,
And kindness to your soul.
To whom in the world

I shall call a friend,
And extend my hands
For my own self worth?
For that you should know
A kind, and gentle soul,
As I.

25.

I Shall Honor the Love

What feelings are real
That love can only speak,
That I will understand,
And speak also…
The silent tears of love?

Sweet Love
Come to my honor,
Bless me with a gentle heart
To speak freely with me.

My gift
Shall feel
The light of this love,
And set you free,
That one day
You might come back to me.

I am in love,
And the power of it
Honors your blessings,
Overflowing my heart
With commitment's song,
The one we sing in April showers.

I am in love,
As sweet April sings to me,
And blessed are the sounds of love,
For I have fallen gracefully,

And my honor
To love you so,
Will be the call to my heart
To sing to you my wanting love.

I am honored
To have loved you,
But praise your love
The way I do,
Says it all,
The honor of your heart
To love me true.

26.
What Light We Shine

Consuming energy,
Grand is the light
That produces one candle power
Within the darkness.

I live in the light,
And sleep in the darkness.

My soul shines bright,
What light I shine.

I live,
That light will enter
Into my soul,
And have my mind's eyes
To see.

I shall hold the light
Within my searching soul,
To bleed the brightness of life.

I hold the candle to my heart,
What shines in the light I see.
I hold it silent now
Into the dark,
To give you light,
And light your eyes
Upon me.

I am the flame eternal.
The gift of wax I bleed
For fuel,
To give the light this
Candle light,
The golden glow
Of a red hearted flame,
That spills light eternal.

27.
The Seeds of Sanity

I look into forever,
For what thoughts we may
Encounter from an empty sea
Of souls that rise.
Arise oblivion,
That has reached an end.
I am not ready for my demise,
As my soul floats in the sea of time.
Where sails grasp upon the wind,
And my eyes follow the shooting stars.
That nothing, could actually be everything
As where I have came from,
Also to where I have gone,
As time holds my soul
For moments upon this Earth.

Close the door,
Its cold outside.

Reaching for the cell,
I become the art that partakes
A room of green flakes
And gray enamel.
Teaching shadows how to curve
And seal the fate of my hidden womb,
As a fetal position upon the floor.

I can't take it anymore.
The hum drum box to scream in,
The vacancy of electron dust
Collecting upon my fingertips.
Such a tasty remorse,
To a plugged in socket.

My apples reach a sight
Of a tube with rays,
Beaming the room
Of a blue tone fad.

I speak,
Therefore I am spoken of.
With sound bouncing about,
Shouting loud into my eardrums
At the beat of my heart.

I feel the ear wax melting.

I crave the simple words,
To hear the wonders of my thoughts.
I save the silent aptitude,
As the spoils of life
Fall unto to my feet,
Laid neatly in rows
Of bedded sheep,
Counted the slumber
Of baked beans in June.

I cherish the words that worry,
And never say goodbye.
These bruises bent hell fire
For shooting off on the Forth of July,
The ones that say hello
When my muted voice replies.

I call upon my attention span,
Wise, where I am weak.
My hands washed clean of crime
What fate lies within my grasp,
That I can venture out into stormy weather
And take action for my fate.
My hands had choked to death,
My words before I could speak.

28.
The Eyes of Truth

As time is gifted,
It falls upon destiny
To become the truth
Of who we are.

I can see clearly
Into the eyes of truth,
Looking into a mirror of myself
To reflect that which humbles upon me,
As I shine away the glossy film
Of a negative of a filthy life.

The seeds that surrender
My breed to a broken heart,
To echo into a valley
Of the many eyes
Looking upon me,
For some sort of gratification
For themselves.

I can only whisper of the truths
That lay wait upon the tomorrows,
For today I have listened well
And nothing was ever said
About the truths of my eyes.
Not that I had ever heard much
In the past of what I speak,
Only to seek for somewhere in time
To see fit my wonder of being blind,

And looking into the eyes of truth,
Looking into my very soul.

As time is gifted,
It is raised upon a pedestal,
To reach upon a giving truth
And give life to my purpose.
Such praise of existence
To see myself in the Ernst of life
Fulfilling deeds of satisfaction,
And looking into the eyes
of an unknown truth,
As I cannot lie to myself.

Chapter 5

29.
The Quiet of My Thoughts

I like seldom seen things
And versatile words,
Speaking sharply
Into ears that would listen.

I like the quiet of my thoughts
When it tells me when to listen,
The words that I love to write down
As the wonder of what I hear.

I compose my mind
Into the meanings of my thoughts,
Of so many people listening,
And the thoughts that are ever speaking.

The quiet of my thoughts
Of being who I am,
And listening to a world
That is touching my soul.

The quiet of a universal scream
Into deaf ears,
And I can hear nothing
But my heartbeat pounding in my brain.

The quiet of my eyes
That are forever yet to see,
As I believe that I am alive
And see nothing to deceive me.

The quiet of my years
Falling to my knees,
Begging for more of life
And for the moments that it shall please.

The quiet of my thoughts
To keep breathing in my hands,
Screaming to the world
What secrets I have heard.

I can hear the quiet of my life
Slowly slipping away,
Into the shadows of my mind
At a single wonder of a day.

I can hear the moments of such praise
In the matters of what could be,
In the choice feelings of my mind
Such sweet sounds of memories.

I can hear the mellow meanings of life
As they cry out in wonder,
The secrets of what I heard yesterday
In the sounds of joy and whispers.

I can hear the sky awakening
Into a battle of the painting brush,
As dawn opens my eyes
To the closing of the night.

I can hear what sleep
The darkness awakens into my mind,
Listening to the world of dreams
And holding to the dark faces of life.

I can hear the quiet of God
Calling into the wind of time,
Wishing for my soul sweet days
To become what Earth I am.

The quiet of my life
To become just a mortal man,
To single out each day for memories
For the quiet of my truths that I shall speak.

I can hear the quiet of my thoughts
To feel the birth of life,
And fall the death away
That comes before I would die.

The quiet of my words
To speak before the day is gone,
Of what life falls before me
In the memories that I have done.

30.
The Beauty of the Life Within Me

The wind will carry
What songs my life will sing,
As it slips through my fingertips,
And I feel faint
Of what life falls before me.

Shy, my soul to fly away
Into a windward pass my life falls fate.
As I fly by my wounded wings,
To fall the content of time.
Into the rising of the sun,
The sheer of open sky.

I hold my hands into the air
As the light shines upon my soul,
What days and nights bring upon me
A life to hold in dreams.
My precious life to fly away
Into the distance of the wind,
That so soon carries me away.

This touch of life
So frail to the mortal wounds that give,
To taste upon me of diamond's glitter
That sparkle of silver in a golden sky.
To praise the beauty of life,
And to feel just a glimpse of time.

Shy away the winded flute
That songs shall sing the ivory eyes,
To cry away the length of time I live
Passing before my very eyes.
I call beloved into the light of God,
As my feathers fall to Earth
And disappear away.

The beauty of life
Can only feel such moments to hold,
To praise the beauty of the life within me
As time so carries me away.
As it lifts me high into the light of God,
As life becomes,
I will grasp and hold.

31.

My Soul in the Shadows of Time

Forever I walk
Into the valleys of time,
Spacing my steps
In the forward of a blind,
My soul forever lost
In the shadows of my life.

I walk silently holding my breath,
Holding my chest to a beating heart.
To see and feel the greatness I have done
For what life I know is to be grand,
An illusion is at hand
As I swallow my words.

Each soul is a shadow
Forever searching,
Into the valleys of time
That we catch on a whim.
Walking silently with truth
And a beating heart,
Silent to the words I weep
For what life I know,
to be the flowing of sand of time.

Time speaks the words of shadows
The walk of life must know,
My soul slows in the shadows of time,
And now I walk alone.
Into the valley of the shadow of death,

Where an illusion becomes my life's shadows,
And I swallow hard my words
Meant for life.

Forever I walk
Into the valley of shadows,
Spacing heartbeats with footsteps
And holding my hands to a beating heart.
To cry into the wind
My sweet shadows,
That life should send me away
As I walk with friends.

32.
The Moments I Have Known of Love

What kindled spark I flame
Upon my desires?
Oh' my goodness
To what reaches the heart,
The same that feels my heart to see,
Such moments this grand of love.

Reach for me
This sky of open love,
That I should fly away
With a windward song,
And strike the heavens for love.

Hold the sacred tongue
That I should speak,
My fire's kindled deep
Into a flame of love.
I am in way of cupid's arrows,
Shooting at the stars with loving eyes.

The flow of love
That my heart beats,
And the dreams of sweet candy mix
Sacred upon the tongue of a child,
To flavor the arrows of love
That sting upon my heart.

The moment of my desire to love you so,
Is the moments I have known of love.

To taste your touch of lips
That lust will cross my path,
And I shall hold such moments
Well within my heart.

The moments I have known of love
Are the moments of my true desires,
That you touch me with a way of heart
And kindled a fire upon my love.
That my heart would speak in loving you
With scent of lilac and rose,
That I should fly away with loving you,
With now a wounded heart.

33.
Silent Spoken Words

As I speak
The words that fade away,
As I write
The wisdom of my words,
They will last forever.
As I am the poet
Of my own words,
And who creates
His own visions in life.

I see the kingdom of my eyes
As the thoughts are all in my head
To explode the life within me,
And I thrill to write down all of what I see.
To create the moments of my worth,
My total of being
Here on Earth.

I feel the truth of living,
Slipping out into the world
And creating a life.
Into new visions that we require,
And I am thrilled to be who I am.
In a world that is so silent now
As I cry out the words of my want,
The wisdom of my eyes to see.

I choice the words
Against the script of life,
Conforming to our needs.
Slowly soothing the pain of life
Within my eyes to see,
To beacon birth as a life force that is
To be recorded with files time.
Silently speaking the truth of life,
For me there is nothing else.

My words lay dormant in the wind of time
As I pick them up and write them down,
And all to see the wisdom of my words
As I lay them down upon a paper clip.
As I cry to weep the tears of life,
And silently speaking my truth.

34.
Time Will Tell

Time will tell the truth of us
Who gently glides the rail of stars.
We breathe the dust of Autumn leaves
Falling to our knees in prayer,
Oh' God,
Grant us the wisdom in a living life,
For we are the ones who care.

Sweet journeys as my soul is content,
My mind is all of what my eyes have spent.
Sending sounds of great fortune
Into the lights eyes of God,
I pray thee well,
Shinning upon the feet of heaven's throne
To unite the ways of man.

Only time will tell
What greatness has for our future to become,
That man, and the glory of God
United under the wisdom of the sun.
I swear by oath of an Autumn mist
I shall breathe of the life I see,
To become what is real in life
And fear the life inside of me,
To love every man, woman, and child.

If I am to be judged
Then what the hell am I doing wrong?
To see such sights of displeasure

As war has wronged our needs,
And carry my heart to the judgment stand
Where I would call my peace with God.

Time will tell
And life will show us worth,
Giving new recognition unto God
Singing verses of song into the sky.
Melting my words of wish and wisdom,
As a gift of helping hands that cry.

Time will tell
As we care for love, life, and mercy,
To give our hands a meaningful life.
As our lips would be sealed
By the visions of our faith,
By the life we so deemed fit
And by the grace of all our inner fate.

35.
The Unique Obsession

The rage of butterflies
Pivot through my stomach,
As the sandstorm days wipe away
Minutes of my life.

I lay upon a stiffened board
From the slab of death I see,
Arise my soul from sleep to wake
As dawn awakens my eyes to see.
Into splintered memories of my past,
One life I lived to cry aloud
For such moments that I see.

I am the father of my life,
The mother of my love.
Once the child who chilled the wine
And drank water from the blood,
Now gathers the wood of bedded bliss
And leaves to fall a pillow for my head.
As memories shallow thinking pit.

My life is a unique obsession,
Where by time is slowly slipping away.
Shows a grand detail of my vast life's meaning
An obsession to live on forever,
Not hoping that I should ever die.

Comes the beggar's entrance thief
Into the sea of time,
Where I gather wood for a free formed life
The only bed that I could see,
Were roses upon the vine.

I am the child who storms this love
The weakness from the womb,
I hold what is so dear to me
With the children of myself knocking,
To take part in this life I love.
For love,
The memories go deep down
Inside of me.

Chapter 6

36.
Fantasy of a Desert Sun

Following the Serengeti
The trail meets with the dusty wind,
And the land is raped
From sunshine and savaged souls,
With the ravage of animals
Caressing the water holes.
Where the villages of mud huts
Soon withered away
Into an evening sun,
Crackling wooded shacks
Fell fate to the cool night air.
The screaming of nature in the darkness
That called upon the night,
Were animals.
From the fear of a child
Who cries the night,
As the snapping of the campfire
Boils into a dance
Of the village spirited souls.

I hear the echoes
Of a lion roaring
Into the deep darkness of the night,
As he roars into the winded flight
Silent screams were heard.
With distant drums
Only to see and hear the dance,
And stories of tribal lore.
As the smoke from the fire

Cooked the nightly feast,
Sweet aroma of sage fell prey
To fold upon the camp,
With a naughty stroll.

Catch the wind of beast
The song of the silver bells,
As the dance continued into the night,
And the dust of dancing feet
swelled the night air.
Into the soft frail fire
That cooked the kill,
And soon the children would wake
To have their bellies filled,
And shouted to be full.
As the sleep within the night
Was the call of a lone star hunter
Creeping to the edge of midnight,
Upon the village sight,
As the wind would blow
With solemn sails,
The sheets of biting cool rain.

The sounds of life
Echo throughout the camp
And flicker into the night sky,
As spark embers float
With a breeze of silent calm,
Upon the desert floor.
To slowing a fall of dance into a trance
About natures door,
And sings gathered souls
Near a firelight stew,
And ring upon the ears of
Nurtured crying babes.
To touch the face

Of fish and foul with a mighty flame,
Calling upon the breath
Of a shouting lion,
Who beds upon the scalp of a fresh kill.
To shiver the ground still with pain,
And stirs the night into a rage
Of a feeding frenzy.

The sounding song of the beating rain
To rapture the souls,
And drip from the shake palm roof
Like church bells ringing on a Sunday morn.
Dancing below the foot
Of a mudded hoof walk,
Splashing at the house of God,
And the faith healers singing praise.
Jumping, dancing, rejoicing
And to bow their heads in prayer,
Hiding within the dripping wet night,
One that nature understands.
That all entities
Fall into a grand scale of things,
And that the tribal people
Were only a few,
Upon a world in numbered thousands.

The voice calls out
As crying ears follow the wind,
Brushing a stroke of ash
Upon the face,
As it sifted sand into the mouth
To bring warmth
From the heated fire.
Who spills the blood of a hooded cow
To make for the child to eat,
As if a mighty horn to sound,

As death cooked the flames
And shouting a dinner bell.
Starving souls to surrender their want,
As children give up their watch
For all to eat.
Slowly dancing a trance of fire
As the light of flames flicker
Into the eyes of sheep,
As they pass away to sleep.

The hunter breathed a song
Of the seven winds,
As the cries upon the night
Were the hunted animals,
And from the darkness
Of the village light
Were fire from flame.
Came a dancing roast
Upon the twist of turning wood,
Providing food for fuel.
That once it could be of life,
As the animals hunt
Each other to survive,
Pray heated feet of a survival hunt,
That feet pounce
upon the throat of fair game.

The chant of passage
From the elders of the camp,
As the younger hunters
Tell of great stories for the day,
And feast upon the prey.
That begged an oath for a hero God,
To slay the night's food
For a hungry child,
And feed the mouths

Of so many men.
Shall gift the send of rain
To growth the desert's dry wells,
And treasures to be found
In a God hunter's eyes.

37.
The Fear Inside Me

I am no different
Than any other human being.
My thoughts are much the same,
My lifestyle much the same,
Yet, I see something different,
As I look upon each day
That I live.

Maybe it is the fact
That I should be dead right now.
A fact of guilt or truth
That cheating death
Is a fear upon my mind,
And a savaged thought upon my soul.
Most like living,
The eternal bonds
That hold me
To this earth.

I am alive
At the grace of God,
And for the first time
In my very eyes-,
I can see the truth
Of things.
I truly feel free,
Except for one small
Detail,
That any day could be my last,

As I can feel death
Squeezing at my chest.

If it were not
For the fear inside me,
I would plan for a great life
That so sets my soul a fire.
But the pain of living
Is a tired thing,
And the joy of life
Sometimes a hopeless thing,
And for this
My fear is real.

As I listen to the music of life
I can hear no evil,
Just the many tunes
That roam upon my ears,
About the hills and valleys
Of my life,
Hiding the fear well inside me.

For fear doth set me free,
The wonderings of
My lust for life.
It does not pain me
To search for
The great revival
That grabs upon my soul,
But to let me go
And abide in me
The peace and softness,
That life should
Truthfully know.

I have need of life
And don't want to let it go,
But the fact of the fear
Inside myself,
A hold of the spirit wise
To control my life,
Will slow the hands
Of earth,
And soon shall set me free.

I face the fact of death
At every step I take,
But life holds for me a place
That only gives to us,
A moment in passing fate.
When we pleasure upon the world,
We must relinquish the things
That we most cherish in life.
As death abides our soul
To come and take us away,
No more quest or grant
Or an evening sun.
As shadows bring us face to face
In dealing with our life,
As our last of visions upon the earth
That bring us to such to this great day.

38.
Bread and Butter Things

Whisper as I cry,
The things
That I want most in life.
The dreams that come and go,
And the many meanings
That have been showed to me,
To feel the bite of reality
Stomping on my toes.

I whisper
When fate comes a knocking,
As the secrets of life
Will amuse my soul.
Sometimes getting bragging rights,
And sometimes filtering rainy days,
For some things in life most wanted
Would be just a little out of reach.

Bread and butter things
That wisp upon a baker's pride
And bakes his pies,
Bubbling stewed apples
And steaming hot peaches,
Dripping with apricot jam,
Mouth watering tastes of seduction.

I whisper things
That I crave,
And my mind

Falls to a total daze,
When I see these things
In my head.
Like willows weeping at the glen
Shadowing the secrets of the wind.

I whisper
Into a paradise of fine treasures,
Where bread and butter things
Can only cash and carry,
Hoping that life will soon
See the sweet joys.
The sweet melancholy,
That holds our dreams
Into a good night.

39.
Praise Be Well

We really praise ourselves
Into the front pages of history.
The goal that we place
Upon ourselves,
Praise be well,
That we cannot forget
These things.

For we are the names upon history
That do these things,
What words we speak
That are so important to us.
As life is laid down
To us on a silver platter,
And we are praised
For the memories of all time.

We grasp at change
And strive for perfection,
Sometimes losing our sanity,
Sometimes choosing the wrong
Roads to travel.
But praise be well,
We are the beings of who we are,
Raining cats and dogs
Of destiny.

I grasp at the straws of life
Begging for no more remorse,

But to endorse my name
Upon the books of time.
Into a catalog of speeches
Sounding the wind,
At any given time,
or any given place,
Praise be well
Of what I speak.

40.
The Greatest Day of My Life

When I woke,
It was like
Being born into the light.
I shouted,
I cried,
I cursed the wind with the words
I never knew I had.

I said,
What the hell now
That I be spoken of,
If I am a sinner
That I would have
A few choice words to say.
Draining my lungs
From the heat of cold's passion,
As I
Shook to a breathing air moment,
To gasp for air.
At the feeding time for tears,
Of the years ahead,
As I swore an oath
To live out loud my somber days.

To be born,
Was a sacred vow.
A shock to the system,
As it had given me joy,
As it had given me fear and anger,

Cold and pain,
Mixed emotions
For a waking heart.
I swore out loud the words
That made me show emotion
From the start,
For the life of me,
For the words,
I was now feeling.

One great day
I was to awaken,
Only to hear the sound of my own voice
As I choked on the surreal of life.
Giving me purpose,
But promising myself
Just another day,
Another moment
Of swallowing life,
And my breathing rhythmic spasms
To a beating heart.
To become the greatest day
Of my entire life,
Just not having to die.

As birth released me
Into the wind,
Into the light of day,
My soul jumped into fast mode.
Life just flew by me now
As the seconds of the eternal clock
Kept ticking,
As it slowly faded away
With time and memory,
Evading my walk with life
As I grew older.

As I lived
Each day,
So shall I fall into the history of it,
To become another great day
In the many days of meaning.
What I lived at this moment,
And who I have become,
That my greatest experience
Would only be
In a moment's matter
For my own self worth,
Truly my own
Habitual self.

I could cry the many tears,
And see the wants
Of my eyes,
As I am born,
So shall I die.
I could scream out life
Into a rage of fit,
For my birth gives me a new awakening
That steals a still born sun
Rising at my wake.
My great gratification of it all,
Being the greatest day of my life.

41.
What Love Touches Me by Morning Light

I am the beggar of my dreams
To hold the night,
To love the early morning dawn.

I understand what dreams may come
To sleep the night,
To wake by morning light of sun.

Crimson wake that shields my sorrow,
Sleep the brightness as the day becomes my borrow,
What stars were swallowed into the night.

What love endures the darkness
That my soul sleeps,
And carries me on to awaken by morning sun.

Enters my room from out the darkness
To sleep the night away,
To bring light upon the storm of day.

Showered stars become the fallen souls to sleep
Knowing I shall sleep,
What ecstasy that this light should bring upon me.

What might I see
That darkness sleeps,
And my soul carries on with death?

To be what follows from the night
Awake I will be,
And surrender not of my eyes into the darkness.

Sleep, gladness, sake of love
To wake upon the rise of morn,
That I should follow the morning sun.

What might the light I see
To wake unto my eyes a burning light,
The light that shines upon my heart and soul.

To bring my burning desires of dreams
To fill the morning spill of light,
With waking stars upon my eyes.

42.
Written by My Hand

What words I will follow
Into the wind?
What shines my day
That I will send,
The dreams upon my world?
I will sacrifice,
The words that begin
With only a flower.

Written upon the wind
That wakes the morrow,
What little words I can understand
That shakes and borrows.
As I the poet who understands
And chooses to write what words I swallow,
And wilt away with time
Those words I gather.

Written by my hand
Would be the scribbles of destiny,
What words I would speak
To write the words of history.
Of all that wisdom that speaks
I have thought now to borrow,
And all that we have listened to
To write all this that matters.

Chapter 7

43.
Sister of Imaginary Friends

My life,
The long roads I keep,
The short time I sleep,
Seeking a heartfelt friend.

Taken,
To where the heart grows fonder,
Awakens the sister of desire,
Never is there ever
A day left behind.

I look towards
The friends I know,
As my life leads me onwards
Into the realms of the unknown,
As I see the sister has remembered,
A time without friends.

I remember,
Without a day of cost,
Most memories I have lost,
Concluding towards now
The time of our end.

Oh be,
That my eyes might shine,
As I smile on another day,
And see the sister
Of imaginary friends.

Oh see,
That nothing is lost in time,
Knowing the truth of all my friends,
Until the day that I die.

Oh be,
That my eyes be wide open,
Not blind to another day,
To the blind side of life,
As I shine my face for joy.

A vision of an angel of mercy,
A sister of imaginary friends,
To sway the scale of judgment
In the wonder of all my life.

44.
Better Choices of the Heart

The way the wind blows
Shows me the way to lean towards life,
What little wind blows
Becomes the choices of the heart.

What little wind is calling my name
That I came to remember time after time,
What whispers were called
For my heart to remember,
What comes calling to my ears.

My heart remembers
A wish for my youth
As though it had passed away,
Yet calling to my years,
I remember my own name.

Choices of the heart
Passing glory days,
To be waiting
Before the edge of time.
I wish contentment
For what has fallen in within my time,
Where by I do surrender and understand,
as remember my name to be called.

By acts of love and compassion
To fall into the world of the living,
That we speak to ourselves

And surrender our souls,
For the grace and dignity of others.
Where by time will tell,
What choices we whisper for life.

A choice of heart
For what life has brought upon me,
As I act accordingly
By the choices of what matters most.
The world presses onward,
As the life we live
Surrenders.
My wish content
For what choices I choose,
In the calling of my heart.

45.
The Luster of Home Grown Love

Some days,
Satisfaction brings upon me
A dwelling place for love.

The light that shines my eyes
Into the nakedness of my heart,
A dream of home grown love.

The wants of all my heart
To covet the dreams of love,
And follow to joy and romance.

I feel a grasp to the luster of love,
Had it dropped upon my lap
And desire my sweetest touch.

A wish upon the fate of it all
That dreams partake in the memories,
By dreams that I acquired.

Where by faith alone I could see,
And gracefully take it to
A luster into the wanting love.

As all I could encounter,
Would be this wish for love
To come and visit with me.

A luster into my home grown love
To prompt a would be desire,
That I see myself fit as a fiddle.

A choice of thought
To truly come from my heart,
The want and matter of all this love.

To bring to me the luster of all the world,
A choice that would truly be my heart
For a home grown love.

46.
Showers of Rare Beauty

Flowers rake the golden sun
Shimmer rays to love at heart,
Where weak the will subsides
Myself to hide,
Beneath the beauty of it all.

Strands of strings for golden hair
Shifts the evening sun to care,
To share within the eyes
Myself to stare,
At the beauty of love.

The sky is the limit
Where great beauty rises,
Where the heart so wanders
To raise the raining rainbows,
so cries tears of beautiful love.

The mountains reach into the heavens
To flair the majestic beauty of earth,
From silent valleys
And crying rivers,
To birth beautiful love.

Oceans shift from shore to shore
And below is evening sun,
That rises upon the full moon glory
And taps at the wizard's shells,
To hear sea sounds of beautiful love.

Flowers flake upon the midnight lace
To hold upon the hands of a human race,
Such beauty of life that is so everlasting
Facing the silent shadows of earth,
To climb upon this beautiful love.

The soul gathers tears of beauty
To hold upon the heart a sacred love,
Such showers of rare beauty
That bed upon a cool steaming ground,
A heart that joys in beautiful love.

47.
The Greatness Will Follow Us

The times are changing
As I am swallowed by bits of life,
And I am consumed over the death of it,
For my eternity is rising from the salt.

I find myself in a losing battle
As I lose my steps within life,
Wondering in the wanderlust of time,
Dusting myself off from the old gray matter,
And fusing bits of memories together.

The hollow of my dreams
Shaken beyond the porthole's cage,
Pitted from the potholes,
And follows me into the shadows
Of a dark and dreary day.

I come here today
That I might lose myself,
Over and over again
Within the errors of my ways.
That the days will pass
As I ask myself over and over again,
About the emptiness of my sorrow,
And how should I act out my life
Between night or day.

That a child is born
And my name moves on,
Rising from the family tree of history
Where every man, woman, and child
Should see themselves with dignity.
But life flows within myself,
And drips into the visions of the past.

Where all of me partakes on bitter battles
That the greatness will follow,
As I find myself lost
In the crust of time, and a pearl palace of place,
To do my own will of living
And spilling out life and love.

48.
By Way of Light

By way of light
I shall see my way,
What light there is
That shines upon my path,
Beyond the shadows
Of yesterday.

Be kind
This light,
That gives me passage into the unknown.
Light,
This beautiful thing
That grasps upon the foot of me,
That guides my very soul.

Light,
That oceans do follow,
As it splashes upon the shores of life,
And gives birth to new meanings.
As we see ourselves shine
In the murky darkness.

Behold,
A light that shines
Into the forever winds of happiness,
Beyond the good measure of time,
That sleeps silent the light of life
Upon the grandness of my soul.

The stars
That light the night sky,
Becoming the eyes of God
In the darkness of the universal wind,
To filter through the galaxy
And blind a moon upon the seas.

Cosmic light,
The blood of God,
That pours within our souls.
The brightness of life
That gives us tranquil life as balmy seas,
Of raining tears of sight from eyes,
To see everything by way of light.

49.
The Color of My Love
[A Song of Love]

[Chorus]

Hay—wave a little kiss to me…
I'm begging you—can you see,
As your dreams are all around me,
And I want to dream a little kiss for me…
With the color of my love.

Hay-
Shake your little booty for me…
I've been waiting—can't you see,
As your dreams fall upon me,
And I want a little kiss from you…
To paint the color of my love.

I

I see it in your heart
The color of this love,
Turning red…
As like a heart on Valentine's day
As red as the love you are,
And your love shine my way
As you look into my eyes…
This sweet color of your love.

II

I want the blue of your sweet love-
The color of this love,
As a lonely heart I do have
And my eyes are turning blue
Always being without you…
As the sky falls into my eyes
My heart is blue for your touch of love
To make it a perfect day
As I see it in your face
The love you have for me…
The color of your love.

III

I see the green of jealousy
Everywhere I want to turn,
As my heart desires your kiss
And my lips are burning fire
And I miss you so like this…
As my heart begins to pound
And the jealousy is all around,
And I'm green with all this envy
I can feel your love for me…
The sweet color of your love.

IV

I dream the purple of your touch
As I'm turning black and blue,
As I'm wanting you so much
And my heart begins to burn
As I feel your wanting touch
And I miss you so…
As my heart begins to burst

To feel your wanting eyes,
The purple of my heart
Tells you true my heart for you,
And I can feel your love for me...
The color of your love.

V

I see the orange in your disguise
As you hide your loving eyes
And you try to hide your love from me
But you can't take it anymore,
And I miss you so...
As orange became my naked sun
I would steal your heart away,
Dreaming of a kiss from you
And I have nothing more to say,
As I feel you loving touch...
The color of your love.

VI

I can feel the silence of your lips
As they turn three shades of pink,
Sing into my wanting eyes
The kisses of your sweet heart
And I want you so...
As the color of your lips
Are touching me like this,
The pink begins to fire
And I touch your red hot lips
With the wanting of your touch...
And the color of your sweet love.

Chapter 8

50.
Celestial Love

The darkness deep
The silent sounds,
As the whispers of God
Create love.
The creation flows
With life,
And God stands direct
And to the point,
As love flows
From his fingertips,
And the earth's gardens appeared.

What love
The greatness of man
Has been put upon him,
That God created woman
For the birth of a child.
The garden was a beautiful thing
As hands were joined in creation,
In the communication of love.

The eternal bliss
Fell from the sky,
As darkness fell
The stars arose.
The wishful hands of God
To birth life
Of all living things,
And love shall show

Between them,
Where life is most sacred.

Where love begins
Within the eyes of God,
To create the visions of life
From out the darkness.
A celestial love
That clings to life itself,
And bare witness
As a child would weep,
As the gardens of life
should fall away,
And the earth
Glowed of energy,
As life became the love.

Silence broken,
And the darkness fell away,
God looked into the eyes of man
And there he saw a woman,
Standing upon the bareness of earth
Giving birth to wisdom and truth.
Yet God made man
In his own image,
And all must love
The face of God,
As woman
Begot the fruits of love,
And given it to God
On earth this day.

The truth
Became the light,
Where love has fallen to earth,
And joy became what love

Could ever be.
The celestial of all things eternal,
And God rejoiced his joy
To all living things.

What love is,
To be from the beginning
To the end of time.
What life shines upon us
Is what God knows
We can't do without.
So we partake
In its ventures,
As we find love
Wherever there is ever any doubt.

We find love within ourselves,
To praise God for all living things.
We find love,
Where most anything has value,
And we find traces of it
In our own DNA.

We are
The celestial love eternal,
For without it,
We are just the dust of darkness
And the silence of space.

51.
The Calliope Waltz

Songs of nigh'
Refresh my dreams
Into the reality of my life.

My soul so sleeps
The song of sweet music in surrender.
My heart does weep
For the harvesting of souls beginning to wake,
To take judgment upon my songs.
I will dance all night long
To the calliope waltz.

To see the humored things
And hummingbird wings,
The sweet beat upon my ears
To wake my weary eyes.
I write the songs in the sound of rubia
And gold shall roll the seas of emerald turf.
To woo the sight of her,
The Goddess of who sings the song of the isles,
And dance with me the calliope waltz.

Away with the angst of fear
That death is near,
And a cold nigh' a coming drear,
I only hear
A song and dance,
As dreams to come.

Singing songs well into the night
To sleep my wounds of life.
Beacons the moon with fair delight
Before I sleep with death.
I shall write the calliope waltz
And keep with the goddess
Who sings with me,
To swear sweet visions
And sounding songs well into the night,
To dance my way with a calliope song.

52.
Hear Me a Poem

The day lazily steps aside,
As my shadow dreams forever inside
Of the days that linger on.

Hear me a poem,
A song that whispers into my dreams.
As the poet sleeps,
A song of his own self worth,
As time casts a spell
Written upon a poet's destiny.

Cry by the light of it
As the stars shine—oh night',
The silver moon turns pale blue
As the wind song dances upon my ears.
As pearl eyes to tear,
My heart to choke upon my words,
As a simple poet
Reads to mother earth.

Hear me a poem
That sings to an angel chorus,
That cries the loneliness of the wind,
That dreams a beggar's dreams.
From a ravaged soul that begs for mercy,
A simple soul who sings songs,
A poet of my trust
Like a diamond in the rough.

Hear me a poem
That says I am alive,
As I cry mercy upon the womb of nature
As the breast feeds and I come alive.
As the lamb that I am
Could only survive at a poet's thoughts,
And that the art shall show me this
My naked thoughts to life should see,
Shall sing
Within a single poem.

53.
Lady Love

Who are we to question love
The simple smiles set upon us by dreams.
Come bring me to her,
This lady love,
My dear,
My dear,
My dear.

You are in fine form and fashion
A true signature of love.
From a woman who takes my sensual whims and desires,
From a woman who adores my flirts,
What love,
What love,
What love.

I light the candles
Oh sweet of love.
At the midnight hours I search and seek.
I fondle,
And I am amazed,
As if there were no surprises
As I would only need
My lady love.

I feel the heat
In the darkness of the room.
I steal the sheets from your naked thigh's
And hold you tightly to me.

Your sweet scent to travel my nose
As I stare at your loving eyes.
To weep for you the wonder and awe of love
Then desire of all my cries,
To hold you,
To want you,
My sweet lady love.

54.
The Quiet Times of Love

The evening sparkles with a fine wine.

With a sunlight flair
As daisies and roses were,
Capped within the bottles of wine,
The snow outside blushing.
As a fire inside toasting,
A window of wonder and pink frost
the ice steamed glass of fog.
To chill a frosty glaze upon your cheeks
As your eyes mellow
Sweet of quiet times.

We sat in silence
As the white moon lifted,
As the sun fell short the naked day,
As snow slowly fell the darkened night lit sky.
As we felt the taste of love
Touch our tongues,
With a crackling fire
Embedded with a white bear rug,
To a celebration of love.

The wine
As tasteful as ever,
Our hearts pumping with desires
Melting the frost on the windows.
Bleeding a bottle
In a bucket of ice,

Silenced in love tears
And blinded by the heat of the fire.
As passions burning embers
Touched our lips,
We drank slowly
The flames of love.

The night we longed for
Slipping through the madness of our fingertips,
Madly insane
With passion and desire.
The sparkle of a wine
To make the eyes gleam,
As we kiss the rosy red cheeks,
The night-
Quiet upon us,
Slowly fades into the shadows of love.

55.

Forever Tango

April is the dance
Forever upon the spring,
To leaf a tree.

Where life will be seen
By the light of the sun,
And joy will be here.

By the light of the shade
Shall shallow the wind,
To dance the tomorrows.

Where upon the tree
April is to be seen,
Dancing the Tango.

Dance the dreams
As painted in virgin oils,
With mixed hues of orange,
And a pallet of blues,
To turn green
In the April soil.

Visions to the eyes
A stroke of brush,
And dreams of tomorrows lust
Wit the hint of honeysuckle.
To whisper upon the heart,
The dance
Of forever Tango.

A vision to a melting tongue
A dance into the darkness of light,
And back into the light
Of dark steps forming,
Too,
Then fro,
With form and fashion.
Absolute, to the two steps forming
To sway the other way,
Holding at arms length,
The tree of life
To bud, and bloom
In April's sight.

56.
The Art of Living

For Joy,
I shall live.
For joy,
We shall live.
Live,
And let live.

So shall I live
All the days of my life.
So shall I live
In what ways seem fit to me.

The past falls
As the future presents itself,
Uniting body and soul,
Time and space.
I am my own free will
Wanting to survive,
Tempting fate,
Ready to contemplate
The thrill that is within me.
Bringing about the truth within me,
To wonder,
As I live.

It is a gift
To become the caretaker of your own soul,
Shaping it into a life form,
And to be about learning as we live.

For something to remember
As we strive to survive,
And suffer the consequences
of our own actions.

It is the art of life,
The art of a living soul,
That we value most,
As life begins.
As we see the heart of creation
Giving into us,
For the grand moments of all we seek in life,
As we fall ill fate of it,
And choice the world of the living.

Chapter 9

57.
A Computation of Scatter Brained Memories

The wild of my memory,
Never ceases to amaze me.

The query of all my days,
Written upon the sands of time.

I have left,
But choices of the good or bad,
Sweet or bitter,
The toil,
The soil
That plants me
In my grave.

I swear
By this weeping hand,
My guise would be sane
To have written down
All my memories,
But the shock of it
Would call upon the words
That would rightfully bite me in the ass.

So
I lie a little bit,
Just a little bit.
To entice you into reading more
About myself,
And the many frame of minds
That I have ever become.

Such scatter brained memories
That all my truths might seem like lies,
But that they enhance my visions of life,
And what I have become.

I will
What matters my ways,
And ask myself
As I ask for nor further distinction,
As life has many opportunities
Of explaining myself,
As the way I have lived.

Maybe, the way I have died,
And as now
Come back to life.

There are no formal introductions,
No formal memories to say,
Nor can I object to any such thoughts
That might incur upon my privacy,
Except denial.

I can remember when,
Out of the mouth of babes,
And all the things that I have done,
Short term memory, or not.

If I were to remember when,
And all the things that I have done,
If I were to find them
And explain them,
I would have to have a security guard
And take matters into my own hands.
I f I told you,
I would have to shut you up.

Really though,
My life has been a few proud moments.
Much of it to be just scatter brained memories,
But I'm still living,
I'm still alive, and dying.

What can I say
except
That life is not over yet,
Till the big lady sings.

Or until I'm planted
Some six feet under,
And the Daisies will be pushing dirt,
And the Roses are laid to rest.
If I get that far,
As the lady of the house
Wants to
Suck my ashes up the Hoover,
And I can't seem to afford
A proper burial.

I thought about being laid to rest
In some far off distant place,
Where no man wants to travel,
Except for a vacation.
Up in the hills maybe,
In some silent graveyard
That the old gold minors had used
In the olden days.

Stick me up an old wooden cross
With my name on it,
And we will call it even.

Oh shout about the memories
All in a days worth.
I keep seeing ghosts of my past
Getting still moving time along.

Seems I have most of life
Under control,
And all neatly tucked away.
Don't much matter now
Except for all my historical facts.

I can still remember when
When in high school,
Chasing the young ladies
And running from them at the same time.

I went and got married,
Had some children,
Had some grandchildren,
Becoming a grandfather,
And getting divorced, and re-married.
And now,
At the prime of my life,
I can honestly say
That I'm just another plain John Doe.

Of course now
I have some books written down
For history's sake,
And for future reference,
AI have a few thousand paintings
Hidden in my closet spaces.
Point well taken,
Never put off until tomorrow,
What you can do today.

I guess that just about says it all,
Except that maybe my life's not over with yet.

Ah, yes
I got one more last thing to say,
Never give up trying to succeed.
Because you don't know what you can do
If you don't at least try.

That's my motto.

58.
The Quiet Time

Chorus A

Dreams it seems
To fall from my eyes...

Chorus B

And In My Eyes
I see you loving me.

Chorus A

Dreams it seems
Coming to me...

Chorus B

Forever Falling,
Forever on your mind
For you to love me.

1.

Pass away my heart
To the one
Who says I love you,
Pass away my dreams
To ever love you
Over and over again...

The quiet times I see
Are the dreams of you and me,
As I hold you in my arms
For all of life to see…

The tears of quiet eyes
Remember all the hurts,
Taking all my dreams
For loving you it seems.

Chorus C

I will reach for you again
As you are holding all my dreams…

Chorus D

And the voices of my aching heart
From the silence when were apart,
To loving you again.

Chorus C

I will sweet talk you again
With the quiet of my true heart…

Chorus D

And Feel the love begin
As we shake away the fear,
And hold you once again.

Chorus A

Dreams it seems
To fall from my eyes…

Chorus B

And in my eyes
I will always see,
Forever loving you,
And you loving me.

Chorus A

Dreams it seems
Coming to me…

Chorus B

Forever falling,
Forever calling to my mind,
Forever for you to love me.

2.

Pass away my soul
Forever in my dreams,
The quiet of my heart
To give you all these things.

The quiet times I see
Are the dreams of you and me,
As I hold you in my heart
And forever in my arms.

The tears of my disguise
Will show you in my eyes,
Remembering how it hurts
And the love for you I dream.

Chorus E

My heart is quiet now
For the dreams I love you so…

Chorus F

By the chance that we exist
Hoping for all of this,
That we will love.

Chorus E

My dreams all fall the night
In loving you tonight,
Seeing your love to light…

Chorus F

By the chance of a moon like this
Holding the shifting hands I see,
I love you more each day.

Chorus C

I will reach for you again
Holding all our dreams…

Chorus D

And voices in my heart to silence
From all the tears we part,
And loving you over again.

Chorus C

I will sweet talk you again
With the quiet of my heart…

Chorus D

And feel the love begin
As we shake away the fear,
And hold you once again.

Chorus A

Dreams it seems
To fall from my eyes…

Chorus B

And in my eyes
I always
See you loving me.

Chorus A

Dreams it seems
Forever coming to me…

Chorus B

Forever falling into your arm
Or forever on my mind,
For you to love me again.

3.

Pass away my heart
Loving you from the start,
From the quiet of my dreams
And loving you it seems.

From all the quiet times I feel
And loving you was real,
I dream of you from my heart
And hold you forever in my arms.

The tears of dreams must fall
When I'm wanting you to call,
Oh I remember you and me
And I wanting you to see.

Chorus A

The dreams it seems
To fall into my eyes…

Chorus B

And in my eyes
I forever
See you loving me.

Chorus A

Dreams it seems
Forever coming to me…

Chorus B

Forever falling into my eyes
Forever on my mind,
For you to love me.

Chorus C

I will reach for you again
Holding all my dreams…

Chorus D

And voice my heart to silence
From the words when were apart,
Loving you again.

Chorus C

I will sweet talk you again
With the quiet of my heart…

Chorus D

And feel the love again
As we shake away the fear,
And I hold you once again.

Chorus E

My heart is quiet now
For the dreams I love you so…

Chorus F

By the chance that we exist
And hoping for all of this,
That we will love.

Chorus E

My dreams that call the light
In loving you tonight...

Chorus F

By the chance of a moon like this
And by the shifting sands I see,
I love you more each day.

59.
It Was a World Away

When I was young
Way back when,
It was a world away,
And I could see forever.

My eyes sent me back to youth
As my heart gave me old time peace,
As growing upon age
These restless eyes see very well.

These eyes do seek my truth
For visions of my youth,
Things aren't what there suppose to be,
Looking back into the past.

When I was young
I had the world on a tall tail spin,
On a down hill slope
And loved it every step of the way.

I greet these days with great antiquity
To allow my soul to rise,
Arise the foolish things
That once were said and done.

I remember the times that I have had
As I was born into a tight knit family
As favor was brought upon me
In growing years to come.

I remember the songs that played my heart
And the dance of laughter around me,
To the lessons of the grip upon life
So soon to let me go.

I can see such sweet memories
For truth, as well as the bitter lies,
The dreams of boyhood into a man
In the world I can only now understand.

60.
In the Company of Shadows

I have spoken wise
The words of ill fated truth,
Becoming the poet of who I am
Who sets the world aside.

Thoughts of shadows spilling upon my eye sight
In the naked light I see,
What lays in front of me to fall short of days
A song of bitter memories.

To play below the tree of life and watch it grow
To hold a second life of sacrifice,
Have not forgotten my age upon life
That death is a still a shadow at the door.

Though the shadows be in front of me
My reach for life is eternal in what I feel,
I am but a shadow of myself living out this life
That I should fill all my tomorrows.

I shall have what shadows mirror upon me
But to dream what fate comes away with time,
The darkness is in a pool of light drowning
To become the shining sun of all my days.

To become alive the shadow's will to survive
A grace becomes my shadow's fate to fill,
I shall see the brightness of my life arise
As I see that shadows become the storms of life.

I am but a shadow of the walking distance of time
Where by fate shall someday take me away,
As life talks to death, and sings love songs
And the shadows become the light of what I am.

The darkness shall soon prevail upon me
Thoughts upon the shadows that life be informed,
I have not forgotten my age upon life's book of pages
That my immortal soul shall soon be set free.

61.
If It Is True

I will climb a mighty mountain
And search a dusty trail,
If love be true.

I will swim the seas of time
And float the seven seas,
If love be true.

I can feel it in my soul
This thing called love.
If it is true,
I am in love with you,
And will forever hold you tight.

I can see it with my eyes
This thing called love.
If it is true
I couldn't be without you,
And gladly give you my heart.

I can feel it in myself,
This thing called love.
If it is true
I would gladly die for you,
To hold your soul against mine.

I can shout it out loud,
This thing called love.
If it is true

Say that you love me,
But you always say it over and over again.

I can feel it deep in my heart,
This thing called love.
If it is true
I will give you the world,
I would give you all of my love.

62.
The Communication of Vesting Words

Sometimes
We negotiate
The speaking of a
Universal language.

Trident,
The sophisticated,
The royal,
For beauty and magnificence.
A journey of words,
To comprehend
What matters most
To a universe
Of spoken word.

What matters
To one's self…is to say.

Opulent,
The graceful,
Arrogant and remorseful.
A walk of the timberline,
A voice of stability,
To counteract,
To comprehend
The diversity
Towards one's self.

Festive,
The behavior,
Boisterous and ludicrous.
A timeline befalls,
Becoming shorter
With the universal guideline
That enacts stability,
And interacts with tenacity,
Upon the fatal blow
In harming one's self,
By hamming it up.

63.
Casting Shadows on Forever

I live by day
By what choice of words I pray,
By what lights my vision
In the eyes of yesterday's words.

I live by choice of words
Pounding heartbeat brain ideas
Deep into my head,
And feel so much alive
As I speak in spoken prayer,
The words I try to disguise.

Casting shadows on forever
From a verse to a crying heart,
A great need for my heart to ponder
What words will keep to a waking heart,
To pick up the pieces of yesterday
From the morrow's edge of sanity.

I can speak within the shadows
Of what happens to my world,
As the wind will dust the ashes
And I feel so very much alive.
But blunder into the mouth of a dragon
As my breath is a faint a fire,
Into glorious energy
The words that trek my sight.

To live
A thousand years my day,
Pray the wind to rock the world
Stepping into the day of walking shadows.
Fear of me to say please
As my breath is a faint of death,
It is to rock upon my world
The casting of shadows on forever.

I live by shadows
What visions are in the sight of my eyes,
As I speak my spoken prayers
And feel so much alive.
I gift myself within a sunny day
As I live by my own shadow,
And wait upon my giving soul
To speak my prayers of light.

Chapter 10

64.
Touching the Heart

Solemn speaks my words
To a touching heart.
Where a heart
Cannot break without love,
Nor fear the heart
To be loved.

Solemn are the eyes
Who looks upon my eyes.
To feel the grasp of heart
That one cannot deny.
Might this soul come alive
To rejoice my love?

I rejoice my love
As solemn words are the vows.
A heart will hold
And words will speak the truth,
That life is meaningless
Without a touching heart.

I rejoice a touching heart
That a heart will speak of love.
Such is this love
That a heart will hold,
To be loved,
And touching my burning heart.

Solemn is the touch
In the words we cannot speak.
A heart cannot take
Without the giving true of this love,
A heart that would hold onto forever
And love that will of which it seeks.

65.
You Don't Have to Be a Lady

FOR WHEN MY WIFE IS WEARY WORN.

You don't have to be a lady
To see what need I have of you.
You don't feel
The desires I have of you,
Searching for your love?

You don't have to see me
Looking into your sexy eyes.
Just love me like a woman
Like a child in my surprise.
As the tears you shed for me
Show me the woman that you are.

You doubt if my love is real for you
So see the pain inside,
And hoping for a moment of love
While your tears are smiling through.
To see the woman that you are
And feel it in my wanting heart.

You don't have to be a lady
To take my love apart,
Longing for a moment's pleasures
As I gaze deeply into your heart.
Just love me like a woman
As I am searching for this love.

You don't have to see me
As a man who truly wants you,
And my smiles upon your face
When you love me into the night.
With your passions of a lady burning
with a wanting woman heart.

If you doubt my love is real
Then just look upon my face.
Just love me like a woman
A moments pleasure I will taste.
You don't have to be a lady
To please my love for you.

66.
For My Love

In times
I shall awaken,
To stir the love that stole my heart,
That love would steal
Be still my heart.

I shall hold
What love would desire,
Into the womb of love
I place this burning fire.

For love is truth
To an open flame,
And awakens my soul
To feel so alive.

A lover's touch
To a flickering flame,
The trees upon a forest fire
Steaming with all our lust.

For my love remembers
That love is truth,
To conquer all
As I quiver the fears of love.

For love is truth
As a rage upon the sins of the sky,
As my love is forever
As kiss in a raging thunder storm.

For my love
Becomes my mated soul,
To fear not the fires of love that burns within
Or the cool of heaven's touch our lips.

For love is truth
As our hearts will glow,
For our love
That time will conquer all.

67.
Not Without Great Desire

I wish it were
The days of wine and roses,
When life became
A statement of love.

What love I could desire
To be a statement
Of my own life.

I desire
What great need,
Myself, and others need
To grow.
What peace should know
In the fate of love.

I feel
For great need
That love should have my desire,
If I should awaken
In a world on fire.

In order
To see my unity with love,
The founding fathers face
A trial of spoken verse,
And my complete
Alert of love.

What great need
We have to sacrifice ourselves
To the climbing fate of love,
That it be
Our desire,
And become of who we are.

A love
That faces reality and emotion,
And brings forth understanding,
And the truth
Of such sweet desires.

68.
Ode to a Foolish Mind

What mind
Shall we bring forth,
That stupidity is blind,
And we cannot see ourselves?

What dreams the night
That we contemplate
The fears of the darkness,
And be overwhelmed by fright?

The soul
That blisters from passion,
Ordained by needs of lust,
And the rape of a society,
From a government
Born of it.

Vex thyself into the void of mixture
Where there is no remorse in actions,
Oh' foolish mind,
That soils the doorsteps
Of his own house.

Crap the needs of justice down the toilet
When in the wake of dawn,
All is at the footsteps of man,
And we can find no ill
To our own faults.

Take the hand that bleeds
And cup the mouth that screams,
That thrills into the nights of living hell,
And remember mercy
Lays upon the doorstep,
And your visions
Await the trials of all our souls.

What dreams the night
That a cool wind blows,
And a mind of a fool
Bursts the bubbles of life,
Into a pool of…
Blood, sweat, and tears?

The fool of a mind,
That cannot hear the cries
Of even himself.

69.
Ode to a Child

The one who stares
Deep into your heart
From a shadowed stairway.
Who sits upon a rail
And sliding over
From head to tail,
With big eyes watching
And tears choking with life.

A child
Content with silence,
Until the tears
Rolled down from the face
Wishing for some love.
As a smile was taken
With a cone of ice cream,
Hoping to make things
Just feel a little better,
As it melts with understanding
Dripping down these dirty little hands.

Little cherry lips frozen from the stain,
Fell into a deep frosty pain.
A child suffering from
An ice cream head ache,
But forcing every bite
Down a long and reaching tongue,
To swallow whole a gaping mouth
Of gathering fuel.

Ode to a child
That represents a care package.
Is gathering a cerebral context
And kneeling for prayer
From the jolly skate shoes.
In a time to abide
With a faker's folly,
To touch away pain.
The cry away of dreams,
If ever the eyes deepen
To race a pace of heart,
That will cross the fingers,
And to hold the small hands
For goodness sake.

70.
Category Speechless

I found myself
What days I had to offer,
As tomorrow I will rise
With the setting sun,
And the dreams
We all seem to encounter.

Sexual notation
With our lives in orchastration,
Life fulfilling needs
With the many visions of colors.
We celebrate the wants
And calibrate haunts,
In unison
With haste and decorum.

Seduction without sexual desires,
A mountain not without risk,
and the altitude is climbing
As the storms may arise.
I have performed greatly upon my needs
Of category speechless.

I once gloried in exaltation
And the freedom of the wind,
My wisdom of Everest
Climbing my mountains to the world.
I rise to the oceans
As I am week in the knees,

Calling in the silence
Splashing all of seven seas.

Now the challenge of the rock
In a hold I cannot climb,
As I dance upon my feet
The swollen length of time,
As I shaft the cliffs of Dover
And scale the rigid sky.

I am what words I have
And have lust no more with what wind I had.
That I have cried on the mountain's climb,
That fame what still my height,
I rise my flags in front of me
And hail to be a conquering hero.

Chapter 11

71.
Come Bring Me a Flower

I shoved the day away
Like anger in a field of poison Ivy.
Holding the vines with my teeth
Gritting the anger from my sleep,
To follow the fields of flowers
Seeking daybreak to bring me spring,
Of what flowers bring me joy.

I rest upon a sea of love
To where my heart is thinking of,
The one who comes to me
When I look into her eyes and see,
The soul that shines above all else
Comes to bring me flowers.

I wait upon the sea of hope
Crossing my arms to hold her so,
As a gift of flowers that follow me
To fall into a sea of love.
Walking deep in a flower bed
She holds me into her hands.

Kiss me a flower
This sweet child of love,
I wilt by fate
For only a day.
What anger passes before me
For the flowers to bring me joy.

To bury me into a field of Ivy
Where death sits upon a red rose,
My love comes to bring me a flower
From the times of breath and life,
Laying upon my casket a red rose flower
A love as sweet as a rose.

I shoved the dirt away
Like anger in my eyes,
So weeps a red rose flower
My love had brought to me,
For me to sleep in a bed of roses
What flowers bring me joy.

72.
The Child

Have favor with the child
Where wants and wishes lay.
This child
Who gives hope to the world
Who has little words to say.

I am a child of the universe
Holding many stars,
On a road to nowhere
Except for where fate leads
As life follows.

The eyes of many crocodile tears
That wept for misery,
On a road to nowhere
As an imaginary whim,
At a loss and carry for my soul.

This child
Is the life of sticky mud.
A gift from God
To sweep a rocking cradle,
Where by be chosen as the little one.

Pains me to fate
To distain my mortal thoughts,
As I am the child
And find myself lost,
Far from the great hopes of the world.

I feel you comfort me
And to weep for such a child,
Filling the space for humanity
If only for a little while,
Where sanity has left us long ago.

I am the child who looks into your eyes
And smiles at a great comfort.
To hold and cradle you
For my time of love,
To seek simple things that I see.

73.
A River of Shallow Dreams

A river shall follow
What dreams I may desire.

Color my dreams
Painted with lilac wonder,
As the night confesses my soul
Without doubt and plunder.

Rejoice
From what light,
From out the darkness,
These dreams that reflect my way,
That seem so real,
Hovering over me
In long time hours.

The darkness brings
Upon the break of wash,
To spill the thoughts of sleep,
Flooding my mind
With streams and brooks.

Come bring my slumber bed
To dream in ocean swells,
To dream a spell
Is to sleep the night away,
With vivid thoughts of cockle shells,
Where weeping willows shadow sleeping eyes.

A quit rest
Is a creek upset,
That tears to the eyes go unrest
And brings rain
Upon the forest of night.

Upon the bed and pillows
To flow the darkness of the night.
Into the eternal bonds of fiction
Holding hands within a sea of melting thoughts.
Upon the shores of awakening eyes
My dreams to be a quiet rest,
Shouting colors of serenity.

74.

In the Hopes of the Father

The days will follow
The shadow of a man,
In the footsteps of him
Who walks a great land,
To fill his shoes
On the shadows of his own soul.

I watch
The sky in stars,
And pray my lord will see
My face that shines in the darkness,
Looking into a bright lit sky.
I will see him
In the shadows of my own time.

I will cry
As my heart will wander,
I will fuss growing older,
Looking into my father's eyes
As joy becomes the breath of me.
To take heed in his wisdom
And mercy in his sweet cry,
As death has come
To speak with him.

I shall sing
The greatest of praises,
And hold his hands
Hearing my own heart beat.

Whispering love and kindness
For the life he has given to me,
As the last words that fell from his mouth,
I Love you son.

I shall silence what thoughts I may
To become words with the father,
And what of faith be still my heart
To sing upon the will of life.
To take heed in his grand illusions of wisdom
And the thoughts of his prayers,
And hold his hope to heal my heart.

75.
First by Choice

The days seem to wander
As my heart flutters,
I have chosen you
Over all others.

My soul jumps to the skip of a rope
To the beat of the falling rain,
As I look into the eyes
Of a long lost love
That destiny would ever so claim.

First by choice in the show of things
Of yesterday's voice,
second by choice in the sound of things
That happen by song,
But I listen to the crying wind
As it wails and boasts out your name.

That once I spoke of your sweet passion
I could never forget you,
A first choice in all my dreams
Come near to fall the shadows of things,
But calling out your name
And never to have seen your face.

We are spoken first for each other
What fate has been, and done,
As I listen to the falling rain
Pitter patter out your name,

As it slaps the sidewalks to the roadway
The wind will be shouting out to your soul.

We meet again in eternal bonds
By first this choice in life.
We will seat the trees of life
And look upon the leaf of names,
And find yesterday's voice
Calling out the first names of choice.

76.
Meanings of the Heart

Where by God
In his infinite wisdom,
Becomes the choices of man
By desire.

Reality speaks to me
To my heart,
And makes it whisper
Such sweet songs in a wonderful life.

The eyes
To love the eternal bonds of life,
To taste sweet life as no other,
Where by the sight of God
We become the light that shines on forever.

A king
Who's staff brings glory,
Rise the brick of pyramids
To rise the storms of defiance,
One God
To the glory of the sun.

Life is meaning
And humanity is chance,
At peace with a sea of lace
Laid upon the land of sand,
As the many stars in the sky
Where sails pronounce the souls of life,

With Kings and Queens
The sun shall rise.

The great one
Who will rule the land.
As life has many stories to unfold,
That we live upon the great Nile.
To meet with death,
And life shall set us free
Within another world,
Another place,
Another time,
To become the same
As what life may have encountered to us now,
To be a king or a living God.

77.
Deception to My Mind

What wake is this
That I cannot sleep,
Nor vent out life
With my soul to weep?

I pity you
Oh myself,
For where have you come
To be in my frame of mind?

By the greatness of my own self
I have fallen into the world of woe,
Where I cannot speak,
Dare I not speak,
But laughter to myself.

At what cost
Do I frame my mind
Into bitter judgment,
Do I deceive myself
And pity my own soul
Upon the rain of thoughts,
Cost be
What my soul desires?

I have forgotten my place upon the world,
I have forgotten myself.
Into the womb of sacrifice,
I have smitten my own soul

And deceived myself.
Before my very own lust,
And be damned with it,
The cravings of all my sins.

I have lost my virginity
Upon the rocks of ages past.
I therefore recollect my intent
Upon the deception of my own mind,
Woe, to encounter it.
My last misconception of my mind,
I beg forgiveness from myself,
As this is my true intent to be.

Chapter 12

78.
San Francisco Native

The city of spiraled lights
Shines a fog bound into my eyes.
A golden sun
To a golden bridge,
Setting the evening light
To a white Chardonnay.

I walk upon the sunset shores
Listening to gulls interrupt my sight.
As the gray sand winds my face
And the rocky shores taste my eyes,
From the touting bridge
Opening the doors to an ocean arena.

The city that never sleeps
As the darkness loomed the hillside streets.
Cables rolling till the wake of dawn
Shadows stepping from street to street.
A street car sounding a bell,
As the doors swing open to the light
And the ghosts of midnight appear.

The surf pounding drums into my ears
The splash of bay to gift my nose.
Slides the north sea shore
As the grotto screams the crabs.
As dragons search the street
Down the hills of China Town.

The silence of a silvery moon
Lays wait upon the midnight bay.
Overlooking a city silhouette
From the darkness that fills the sky,
Lonely creatures to stir the night
Where ever becomes the dawn to rise.

The city shines a golden tooth
From hill to rail the trolley sings,
And the sounding of a street car bell
As ants upon the slope march free.
The cool, brisk morn to rise and shine
And fog swallows whole of the sun.

79.
Conscious Thoughts

In dreaming the daylight hours
We sleep the dead of night,
Raising butterflies and flowers
To the sheets that smell of white.

My dream
Is to sail the evening sun,
Across the green spread of land
Into the hands that flowers that float.

Waving wings of feather bedspreads
From a sun of orange and yellow,
to sail the rain that showers the earth
In deep the green of mustard flowers.

Sail on
My sweet conscious thoughts,
With beautiful wings to touch the sun,
As death awaits the darkness.

As the flowers sleep
and all the greenery begins to fall,
I call all the butterflies to gather together
Around the ring of a setting sun.

Sleep the eyes of life
To fly away the wind of midnight sail,
To glitter diamonds of dew drop life
Into a glowing red Ruby sun.

Sail on softly night goodbye
Sweet darkness of golden rays,
So sweeps the sleep into a harvest moon
As the sun drops behind the hills.

Crest the evening sky with butterflies
As death shall swallow sleep,
A darkness that looms of forever now
As the butterfly sails away.

80.
Shades of Truth

The Quiet comes
As the darkness enters form.
A wish for the silence
As slowly sleep begins,
With slip away hours
Time to close our eyes again.
A wish for truth
In a soul that waits upon the dark.

I see well beyond night's image
Awake, my eyes shall see.
The might of the mighty linage
Forms truth to the light that fades the sea.
To dream of ecstasy and romance
What a truth this dream could be,
That combs my hair in the darkness
As feather quill that falls upon me.

I feel the feather bed
Sweet sweat the morning's light.
I skeet the felted sheets that cover me
I stripped from head to toe.
Upon the layers of plucked feathers,
That gather high into a sleeping room,
Where once a leaf spring sat in curls
To find the pea that awakens me.

Where fate has fallen upon my feet
I sleep the gentle soul that sits my bed,
To stir once maybe every hour
And curl my feet upon the wooded head.
Soul's glide into my closet of dreams
I shall shun the darkness with all my teeth,
That the bed does not make me sleep or rise
But ponder the truth of these many dreams.

I see the darkness about me
But I have the many visions upon my fate,
As truth has not yet told me lies
What the darkness holds in fate.
As the stars will never slip into my eyes
And the moon that shines upon my dark lake,
I feel that I must awaken
And wonder of what truth that awaits.

81.
In Interest to Me

It is truth that abides
The wisdom that follows me,
Far into the shadows of my past,
Into the shades of a world gone by,
To tame my very soul.

I have locked the doors behind me
Searching for a brand new life,
Opening the doorways and windows
Just trying to survive the night,
Maybe a glimmer of hope
Or a thought of a wonderful love.

I shall follow truth
And obey my own self deeds,
To come and tell me now
That I believe in the wisdom of my truths.
As in the interest of my ways
Into the shadows of a world gone by,
Far past my views of joy
What dreams I am to hide.

I am the novice
And the master of my own truths,
To be home in a world of my own
As I peek, so shall I seek it,
Of interest in only to me.
As I bare the fruits of my vines,
Drink hardy the graceful wines

And favor the many good fortunes,
As so I seep and keep it.

I rise to see new resolutions
In a barnyard of crowing roosters,
Sitting on a white picket fence
Counting pence and penance.
For my own sins to be set free
As it was of interest to me,
As I grit my teeth to the pain of my eyes,
And would crown myself king
Of kindness and good fortune.

82.
Life in Its Best Interests

We all see life
In different ways,
Though, we are much the same.

I fell to my knees
Feeling the world around me cry,
Why, worry, and crazed
In praise and awe.

Life is so demanding,
Kind of like
Checking in on love,
Or rocking the boat
Of life.
We all have our basic needs,
Wants and wishes to be applied
To supply for many an hour,
For dreams and other things.

We are only human.
Time is only an illussion,
It seems that we work for it
In the many of yesterdays
That life throws upon us.
We work for bread crumbs
That are tossed upon us,
Sometimes,
We take out the garbage
Without really asking why.

Sometimes, we just fake it
And toss ourselves into a reality script,
Not wanting to do anything
At all,
Except vegitate.

Sometimes we really
Feel good about ourselves,
Other times,
We are so careless,
That even a child
Could see through us.

Always bailing ourselves
Out of trouble,
Waiting for the next day to come,
To receive new feelings
Of a day gone by,
With many such
Pat on the backs,
And not having to reply.
We work,
To survive the crumbs
That others have tossed to us,
We take without asking,
And we give without taking.

Sometimes, we just fake it,
And saying things like that we are
Having a good time,
But in reality,
Life really stinks.

The children,
Sometimes,
Just don't listen to us
Anymore,
And we're always bailing them
Out of trouble,
Or trying to beat it
Out of them.

Saving grace,
By saying,
What's the use anymore,
And why we have all these
Crazy hang ups,
Saying,
You know,
I could have had it
So many different ways,
But chose to do it
This way.
I could have been
A person in charge
Of my own life,
I could have been a contender
To the due process of living.

I can always see myself
Doing something,
Weather it be right or wrong,
At least I tried doing
Something about it.
What the heck,
You don't know
What you can do,
Until you at least try.

Sometimes, the life we live
Seems so boring at times,
And on other occasions
We can't stop the many
Meaningful things that happen
On a daily basis.

I like the way
Life handed me things
On a silver platter,
Living out the suprises,
That I would guess to happen,
If I had the hint
Of seeing it
Before hand.

I guess it could
Have been a judgement call,
On what reality would bring to us
On a daily give and take,
Just a little thing
Like love to show up,
And tell us how lucky
We really are in life.

Just little things,
The Great American Dream
That everyone keeps talking about.
Just little things like love,
The love of money,
And a brand new car,
Or a house.

Heck, we never
Know what life is
Going to dish out to us,
Or what could happen
At any given moment.
We could get hit by a car
And die tomorrow,
Or catch a deadly disease,
And pass it on
To the rest of the world.
Or just have a heart attack
And die.

Could be dead by tomorrow,
Could be
By the end of the day.
But who cares
Besides anyone else
Other than you,
And you really give a shit
By this time,
Because your making great money,
And your not drowning
In your own stew.

What the heck do I care
What Bob is thinking
Next door.
Or trying to compete with the Jones household,
Next door at the corner house.

What the heck do I care
What the average Joe blow
Is thinking.
And why would I care

What he is doing,
Or how he is doing,
As long as I am
Getting my fair share
Of life.

Life's a bitch sometimes,
And sometimes
You just have to be a bitch right back.
But remember your health,
If you have your health,
You have everything.
When your health is
Going down hill,
Your really going to be
In deep shit.

So as I see it,
If you have your health,
Then you have everything.
As I see it,
That life's the same
For most of us.
Life in its best interests
Is how we all see it.
As how we feel it,
As we contemplate
Its many wonders
And meanings,
And use it
To the best of our
Advantage.

83.
The Truth of Me

I feel myself
Facing an open wind upon my face,
And I open my eyes to see
The truth of me.

I am what I am,
What will I am,
To become the mortal of a man
Who has touched the earth.

I feel,
What I feel,
To which is my heart's desire,
So much more in life
That what I could ever feel.

As my heart begins to speak,
I feel life tugging at my feet,
What I feel
Is the truth of me
Trying to get out.

The greatness of a man
Is the amount of friends he has to show,
And whom will speak for you
For the truth you are.

I feel myself
In the common of life,
Where the wind blows
And where every man is wise,
As I open my eyes
To see the truth of me.

84.
Identity Note

For where hast' thou taken
Into losing thyself,
If it not be within the mirrors of truth
Where life comforts itself?

Where should I look
Where as such a vision requires,
A note to know who you are,
And to yourself be true?

Positive to negative,
As opposites attract.
Of man over woman
Or brains over bronze.
By water, or by sand
Shall time seal the fate
Of the hour glass.

I am he who speaks the wind
Knowing truth as my last breath.
I am the hand of sorrow
And the sweet smell of success,
Bidding for time
In a vision for life.

I am a soldier
In a war he does not know.
For the greatness to myself
Where time has told me not,

Myself only for a matter for be.
Who speaks of beloved truth,
Bidding for time
As old age sets upon his life.
I am a shadow keeper of myself,
For when the mirror looks upon my face.
The embodiment of a spirit,
Where faith has taken hold.
I am Judas the blemish,
As I am Noah of the floods.
I am the brilliance of a man
In the fate of his short lived days.

Chapter 13

85.
Rise and Shine

The joy in life
Begins in waking up
In the morning.
The wake of life begins
As we rise and shine.

Oh silvery chested dove
That wakes my eyes,
That flies by night
With open eyes,
Please feel free to fly
Into my doorway opened wide.

The golden hordes of Isis
Is the sound of sleep,
As she stretches across the sky
In the wake of stars.
For dreams to come
And sights of treasures
To encounter,
As I rise and shine.

Oh jest me not
Of my pardoned dreams,
With thorns of briarwood
And a melting horn
To wake my ears.
To crest the crown
Of life for me,

As I open my eyes to see
This life before me.

Bring the sound
Of a thousand doves to fly,
Rise and shine my life away,
To hold it upon my heart.
This fortune that must be wrapped,
As a magical kingdom of verse.
I swear by oath
That I do covet the
Many dreams of life,
Of dreams that I awake,
Rise and shine.

86.
The Nescience of Vigilance

We strive to perfection
In order to perform.

Frequent are the miles
Laid of law and land.
The miles of anticipation
Or the dreams that we require,
With a somber attitude
And a joyful reflex.
Calling mortal songs of life
To perfection.
A perplexed jubilant stride
Of vigilance
To support ornate views.

To sweet the pot
As the soul runneth over
When life becomes the soup,
And we eat a hearty bowl.
Lavished in pride
And languished in virtue,
To capture the innocence
Of life,
As it is a beautiful thing
To sing upon the heart.

Oh joy
What the eternal might bring,
To clasp upon the trials by day

And the trails by night.
Where once the dreams to come promise,
A pounding surf of ocean tides.
My true beginnings of birth
And lustful patterns for life,
That I gather upon my days of youth.

The ness of all perfection
To become the mirrored halls of life,
And fate to bring upon a pedestal
A laugh for symmetry's fate,
To nurse a cry for ecstasy
To upon a small planet
Of all the weeping stars.

87.
Composition's Rise

I find myself
When all is lost,
And I loose myself
When all is found.
I find myself silent
In the shadows of time.

I write for the books.
I seek the said words
Under my feet,
Those that bring me sadness,
And those that bring me joy.

I feel the words speak to me
As art painted on a board,
Where compositions rise.
I feel the words of life
Lay upon my soul,
To write them
Into my books.

I write
As a composition speaks,
Gathering bits of history
For one man's given sake.
I rise
To the occasion,
Where life meets the words,
And I can see
A vision of time.

I rise to see myself
Intertwined with the possibility of living,
A composition of matter forming words.
To be
A choice of words,
Who,
Myself, am the gladness
For what forms my speech,
That I am alive
And writing words to keep,
In the glory of my time.

88.
Stepping Stones

The walkway to the garden
Has a footpath of many flowers.
My rose,
To a gathering of stones,
Such stepping stones
For love.

Wide the heart
And the eyes that glow.
A love that smiles
In a world that knows.
For a kiss to feel
What love comes to my heart.
To walk
The stepping stones of love.

In the garden of love
For my eyes to see,
The heart that glows.
Your touch of sweet lips
you kiss with,
And hold yourself
Over the stepping stones
Of my heart,
To fall into
A garden of love.

My heart to beat
The pounding of stepping stones,
To sweep the feet upon the path of flowers,
And gaze my eyes upon the pathway.
My heart so wanders,
These steps to touch.
My heart to wonder,
Sweet the love
The flowers
Gather,
Round a stone.

89.
Fear No Friend

I have lost my way
Into the forest wild of life.
Lost of friends
And touching base with life,
To become a hermit crab
In the shell of a house.

Who shall learn
To speak of friendship?
Mute
Of the soul
That once was,
Now calls upon the many
Friends of time,
To gather
And play together,
Just one more time.

I feel
Lost in the comfort
To hold the hands of another.
Spacing like birds to a wire,
Shifting,
Turning wild in position.
To return,
Then speak
As a friend speaks,
Lost upon my virgin ears.
To cry,

And to swallow whole my pride,
And give way to fear
to find such a friend.

In such need
I dare,
To ploy and sacrifice myself
Into the friendship of another,
Gaining
In such need I swear,
To love
Such a friend
Until the end of time.

90.
Adrift

So Sails the soul into oblivion,
As white clouds explode into the sun.

Adrift.
My familiar,
Into the storms of life.
The pouring shore has lifted me
Into the horizons of youth,
That my eyes have gazed upon
At many times before.

The sea swashes
And land can be seen.
But I boast of sailing
This freedom into the wind,
Silently rocking and rolling
As in the distance of the fog.
With my eyes closed,
And I whisper prayer
Into the service of my dingy.
As the rim of the boat,
is my dignity,
Casts sail
Into a whole hearted wish.
Adrift.
My sail awaits
And I am weakened by the winds,
And I find myself lost
In the shadows of confusion.

From space and time,
Listening to the shores,
Slapping the winds upon the rock.
Feeling the wet of salty mist
Lay wait upon my face.
The cool damp sky
To rise above me in waves,
Touching my throat
As I bite in haste the teathered strings
Of fear that lace upon my doomed eyes.
All sails the fear inside of me
Consuming the fires of hell
As it hesitates my turning back to shore.
Exhausted from the swells
To what fate might exist upon the bow,
Or maybe the stern,
As my cold feet
And cramping hands,
Share the coming chill
Of the dark, night sky.

91.
Ghost

As I see the shadows of life,
I see myself.

I feel the cold of death
As it lingers upon my soul.
I feel the cold of biting fingers
As it grabs my legs and toes.

I feel the lonelyness
Of sweet days and sorrow.
Of a day
That slips away un-noticed,
Pegged to be borrowed
In the land of tomorrow.

I am a ghost
That looms with time.
Into the distance of a living hell
Or a close nit life,
That lives upon the past
And seeks future bonds.

I look into my melting hands
And fear no fate,
As I have already fallen.
Into a fade of my own,
And seeking lifelines
I slowly expand the fears
Into tears of fright,
What might be so.

The tears of tomorrow,
Pitted upon past representation
Of a dorment life form.
As the life force of the spirit
Dwells within the house
Of the living,
To be silent
Into the stills of time,
But brace for eternal
Haunting.

I am a ghost
What fear inside me grows.

Chapter 14

92.
The Morning Flower

She whispers silent
In the call of the wild.
Closing my eyes,
I can hear
The flower drum song.

She speaks to me
In early morn,
With smiles adorned,
To take me away
Into the dazzle of the sun.

She grasps at my wrists
As I pluck her from the ground,
And I sniff her sweet scent,
As wonderful lilacs grow
Within the rose bush thorns.

She needles me
Into submission with sore beauty,
As my eyes rise upon her
Sweet pedals of softness,
And I touch her inner beauty
With a kiss,
Where upon
My lips become numb.

I taste of her sweet flavor
As the bee' busy body
I shall be,
And quench my thirst
Upon her bosoms,
And trail a licking tongue.

The mist upon her eyes
Fakes a cry upon the morn,
And I take her
Into my folding hands,
And wipe the tears away
With the pleasure of my nose,
Smelling the life within her
Melt deeply into my soul.

A flower
That quietly awaits
My arrival,
Then opens to a daylight sun,
And shines for me
All her eternal life beauty.

I silently reach
Upon the guilded pole
That hangs her high into the air,
And wrap my fingers around her
Sweet white lily cheeks,
And touch her under the skirt
Of her earthen ware,
And hold her there
For my arrival
Of whispers to her tears.

She is my morning flower
And brings the day to beauty.
When I rest upon her grassy soil,
And I stare into the daze of sunlight,
Only to feel her breath upon my face.
To kiss me on my nose
With her wetted cheeks,
Where her whispers
Are to love me.

Sweet love
Of a flower,
That sends me
Into a rage of bliss.
Where by
I take her by the wrist
And wrap her upon my soul,
To shout to the world
That I truly love
This flower.

My thoughts of her,
My moments with her,
With such a beautiful flower.

93.
For He Who Knows

I know not
What essence my dreams become,
But to shower me
With the beauty of life
For when they come.
As I am asleep
As they flow through my head.

For chance
Is the greatest of wisdom,
By far
The only thought I keep.
I know nothing
That is worth its weight in gold,
For what the dream keeper
Keeps under lock and key,
Imprisoned by the locks of iron,
Where once gold and silver hid.

What thought that I,
Should take upon the world
Of wisdom and truth,
But now to see
Dusty fields of iron and lead
Or rusty nails holding my bed,
Protruding through the palms of my hands,
To greet my great speech
Upon the world,
As I seek from wisdom's path.

My diversity shall show
What to say to all languages.
My solitute
Could be my justice for tomorrow
The meanings for what my world requires.
Where by
Only my soul,
Could possibly speak
My own path,
And I cannot know the meanings
For the rest of the world.

94.
Chopin's Chase

The stream
The mighty rivers bed,
Sing
To the world of music spread
To seal the sky with love,
What a wonderful place to die…

Write to me
A letter,
So that I can understand much better
The reasons for me to die
As I have lived to write the music,
What songs you may have heard
Flowing from my ears,
This moment to be clear
In visions,
That I fade away too hastily.

Let the world know
That I have listened well the sounds
And wrote them down
To capture the sounds of life
An give I chase,
To my immortal soul.
Sounding trumpets into the air,
And violins to soothe my beast,
So soon shall I die,
So unaware.

Great life that is worthy
I speak to you in music,
As the piano plays for us
These tunes of love.
I chase the dreams of life
To love the way I do,
And love you too.

Pray for me.

95.
The High Pitch of Harmony

I can hear
The music floating in my ears,
This high squeal of a violin
Ringing in my head.

It sings to me
The praise of all music,
And songs follow
The shifting day.

The high tones
To bring me a shiver
Of white and gray,
In a land of colors.

The why,
To ask me
Of what day it is?
Then it tells me
Its only Sunday,
And we are singing
with the choir.

I feel the voice of music
Asking for me to sing.
Require my soul
For a few moments
Gathering high notes
That sail the wind of time,

And fall within my ears
Like a floating vestage of pearls.

The sound of singing sirens
To run into the heart
Of a deaf and dumb person,
Where blindness cannot see
The vibrations of the wind.
As the soul shakes and quivers,
And I can sing
With the want
Of water flowing,
Or the wind howling,
As my eyes meet
The darkness of night,
And I feel the notes gather
As they slam upon my face.

I hear
The high pitch of sound,
That calls me into the visions
Of colors climbing the walls,
And I let loose my kidneys
As my ears roar with sound,
And trumpets burst the sky
Of melting clouds,
As I wet all over myself.

I hear
The high pitch of sound,
As the harmony within my soul
And the wind will flow,
And I chill out the factors
Of sweet lace.
To meet the grace head on,
That calms the beast,

And holds my heart
To soothe my fears of life.

I am the sound
That the music plays.
The words that time forgot,
Fallen from yesterday
In a Winter's daze
Or a Summer's scorch.
As I lay upon my back
Counting the stars in the sky
To catch a glimpse of the sound
As it rolls from my voice.
That I murmur
The sound of music,
That I feel free
Inside myself.

It is time
That sounds my ears.
Into the high pitch of harmony
That gathers beneath my feet,
And I shall hear it
In a moment's passing.

96.
A Pebble in a Desert of Sand

My head hurts,
To be thinking
Of such things.

My mind goes blank,
As I try to think of such things
To make me grow.

As only I would know,
Like a pebble
Sifting through
A mountain of sand,
As only I would know
Who I really am.

My head
Is a pebble
In a sounding surf
Of nightlit stars,
Rolling in a desert wind,
As sand has shaken
Into a mold of life
And fallen upon my words.
The ones I shall not speak
Without the wind to rise,
And ripples the sand
turning a north point breeze,
Crossing the winds of life.

Lake sand
Pouring through
The forest of an hourglass.
My head feels so faint,
As time drips into a bottle
And I count the grains of days,
And I cast myself into the sea of time.
Where life is an ocean
On sandy beach of soil,
And all my hopes float
Upon the winds of time,
Beyond the measures
Of all men.

Myself,
I cannot see a desert run.
But the stars
Do not feed a desert,
When I can reach my hand out
And catch a grain of sand.
Or hold my head
Into the sandy stars of sky
To blister away my pride,
And slowly wither away
Into an ocean's tide.

If ever,
The desert runs deep
With running sand,
And my hand
Fills the hourglass of time,
To fill deep from within my eyes
The tears of sand
That fate spills upon my life.

If ever,
I feel the need of life
Beneath my bare feet,
As the sand is hot
And running through my toes.
I feel the need of want
Piercing my head
With the bones
Of time
That wither away,
As the sand melts
To make the hourglass of life.

My head
As a pebble,
Rolling into the sand
To count the many wishes of life,
Or the stars mounting into space.
Where I can see forever
This sand that seals the fate of time,
To think grains of sand
Mounting within the glass of time,
To blow away once,
And gone forever.

A desert of sand
That a child must play,
A cat must shake away its footing,
This beach where I belong.
As it slaps the waters
To the shores of life,
And I become the shifting sand
As the pebble looses sight.

97.
The Little Wind That Carries

The child visits
As he is to be seen,
And not heard.
As the words
Cannot be seen,
Carried into the wind.
My eyes cannot visual
The time that I spend,
But my alertness
To know that the words
Will someday flow.

The little wind that carries
The life upon a limb
Of a family tree.
To sail the seas of loneliness,
Comes to visit with me.
As a ghost within reason,
A toast of all seasons,
Ticking time on my desk,
For I to notice him.

He would visit with
The quiet of sound.
He would prefer
That I be around,
Who has come to me
As a ghost.
Within reason of course,

To know that he is there,
For the sounds that he makes
Is very clear,
And doesn't hesitate such movements.
As to become part of me,
Just a simple thought
As a voice of the wind.

This child who comes
Weather it be day or night,
My loneliness turns to sorrow
As I feel this child of fright.
That I do not fear
But spare my feelings
Into a domain of thought.
The life enters
And tells me things of thought.

The grasp of life
From a little known wind,
From whence unknown this child
That breathed upon my face.
To reflect a moment of time
Or this parting of space.
Or a parting soul
Who has come to say hello.

I will honor this visit
Knowing that I cannot see,
What stands before me
Whispering into the wind.
But for the life of me,
This child that comes
To touch my soul,
My mind,
My heart,

As I wake upon his arival,
And wait for him
Days on end,
As to when he announces himself
To my curiosity.

The wind that calls upon me
And choices my name and friends.
A child that sees a friend in need
Who has come to communicate
Beyond the grave,
As only he knows how,
And spends his time wisely,
And himself is haunted
By the act of death,
And tries to summons me
With his tricks of the trade,
This ground that I take
For my living soul.

His reach to touch my heart
And to hold me by surprise.
Until I understand his simple wants,
And the wind speaks to me
In a silent voice,
To calmly breeze my face,
Giving me the friendship
Of a ghost.

98.
The Holly Falls of a Floating Sparrow

May the wreath of time
Take a stand,
The sound of a champion
In a naked land,
The olive leaf
To hold a most sacred a game.

A sparrow
To fly away,
As eagles dare the wind.
As the holly floats
Like feathers down to earth,
The wind drips blood and marrow.

To reach the sky
Of an eagle's search,
For the one who got away.
That a fleeting flight
In a sparrows search,
Brings upon us
The days of games.

For the folly
The holly was placed,
But to the wreath of an olive tree.
Crowned champions,
Put upon the head
Of a hero.
The champion's ring of fire

To face the faith of golden gods
Of the plains of Olympia in Ellis,
In the honor of Zeus,
And poetry was read
For chosen games of the gods
On Mount Olympus.

An olive branch for peace
A sparrow in the sight
To touch the torch of fire.
To start the games,
The eagle awaits,
The omega call
Just upon the horizon.

A sparrow in flight
To hold sight of the eagle,
Where the gods and man unite
Under the thrust of honor,
To beg no mercy of a runner.
The holly waits
Upon a gathering bush
To seal the fate of others.

The gods place the odds
To the distance
Of land or sea.
To be the masters of a race
Holding the wreath upon their heads,
Said champions of all the world.
To stand and salute to Olympus
The gathering gold of peace,
As holly foots a ground
And a golden sun to raise the eyes.

The holly falls of a floating sparrow
As the eagle fanned the sky with gold.
Comes the champion's wreath
Upon the head of a hero,
The master of the games
Once a fleeting sparrow,
Now bold and beautiful
To an eagle's wings.

Chapter 15

99.
Desire

What Hath fire
That burns my desire,
Into the winds of destiny,
That flows within my veins,
That the pain of life comes,
That I can call it love?

The howl of the wind
Answers true to be my friend.
What speaks for desire
To be my own mind,
My wants,
My visions,
My turning soul?

It is he who speaks
For me,
The desire that is put upon my life,
Deep into my festered mind,
The cries of love
From a warm enduring heart.

What choice have I
This golden touch that holds my heart,
To seek the horde of love?
As it is cast
Into a sea of time,
That I would beg upon my knees
The giving,

Of just one sweet touch of lust.
My fame or fortune
To be brought before me
And touch the fire.

The toying in my childhood
Where once
A growing man must learn,
And seek its forbidden fruits
And the passions it requires,
To fulfill the needs of desire.
To hold true to love,
Where my mind probes the heart
This feeling of a gut desire.

100.
I Pull Life into Myself

I reach my arms into the sky
Grabbing at life with my fist,
The blinking of an eye
For what life I would miss.
To the glory days
That I would confess my sins,
And fall into a butterfly's maze
From a flowered field
Of sweet oats.

I reach out to grab life
From out the shadows of lasting birth,
And pull it into my own ways of life.
To wrap all things around me
That cover the naked part of me,
That I am the life within myself
That cries humble for sacrifice.
As I hold dear with my own truth
That I am the life,
And the love that I feel.

I pull the life from out the clouds
And into my eyes the sky must melt,
For the search of life has ended here,
As I taste the tears of love
That roll from my face.
As I lace my fingers into the clouds
Pulling free
This sweet touch of life I know,

And I cry for joy
As I live with the gift of life,
As it glows upon my face.

I pull what life is hidden in the clouds
Into my inner heart that beats life for me.
For a mortal's comprehention,
For the moments of sweet recognition,
As I am falling old,
And the future holds no grantees,
And I wish to encounter
So much more of life
Before I die,
And fly away with the butterflies.

101.
Scream

I scream
That you should hear me cry,
As ever I would cry
With loudness into the wind
As the clouds roll by.

I will scream
Into the winter's winds
And wonder why the rain
Falls upon the earth,
As my voice
Falls upon the destiny
Of the sun.

My voice
Has a loud silence,
That when I weep
It is the tears of forever
That fall upon my feet,
As I would drown out
The sweet sunlight.

A voice that could silence
The earth into shadows,
And choice my views into the wind
As it washes upon my face.
To make my tears flow
From the shrill laughter,
I once bellowed.

I scream the silence of what I feel
To see the naked part of me fall from the sky,
And cover the world in a great upheavel
And hear my words cry
As the wind cast destiny upon my face
Just one more time,
And I lay in agony
At the feet of mortal men.

I scream
That you should listen to hear me cry,
And I am not alone in the world any more.
Nor would I be alone
If you should listen to hear me cry,
And that is the moment
That I would surely need a friend.

102.
And All the Birds Were Singing

I hear the distance of the laugh
Of a mockingbird,
As it rolls out a voice twice told.

I hear the sweltered snap of an old crow
As it sits in a tree next door,
Squabbling with a mate
Over stale French fries found on the ground.

I hear a red breasted Robin
Singing on a backyard fence,
Flying over to the nest on the porch,
While baby birds were chirping
From a rain gutter.

I hear a yellow bellied sap sucker
Bleeding a tree free of blood,
At it wanders away to the sound
Of a misfired truck,
Down the street.

I hear a blue jay pecking on a frosty log
From what a blade of grass would filter
In the early morning sun,
And what a filthy dog had left on a stump
The night before.

I could hear the singing sparrows swoop
The morning light of the screen door,
Looking for a meal in a bird feeder
To swear a house was there.

I hear the singing buzz of a hummingbird
As it gathers around a bottle brush tree
Looking for milk and honey,
and diving through rainbows
Of a water hose pouring
To thirsty plants.

I hear the songs that birds sing
Bathing in a house with no shame,
Looking for their next meal,
Maybe worms
That early birds trail.

103.
End of Days

For myself to salute farewell
Is not the words I pray.
But to listen
To what I have to say,
Might mean farewell,
And see our end of days.

The time before
I was born,
God asked me
"Child, when shall you be born?"

I thought about this for a while
And answered,
Not at the beginning of time.
For I cannot see further back than this,
And time shall stand still,
Till tomorrow's blooming.
I would wish to fill in
The many days of man,
As he has chosen upon his goals.

Not in the middle
Where life seemed so backwards, sometimes.
As I cannot see living
Without lusting for more of life
That I could ever know,
Or would wish it to come,
Losing sight of what I would already have.

So shall I answer to God
"not until the end of days,"
For whence I shall see everything
That man has made,
And visualise his every whim,
And find myself in the must of everything,
Before I die.
Then shall all things
Pass away before my very eyes,
Complete the life of will,
And I have seen it unto the end.

I was born
Under a passing star,
One that gifts of wonders,
One that lasts of wandering days.
The days that seen my life
Under a great and mighty sun,
And now I am getting old.
But life has given me so much
Before my very eyes,
And all the days of my life
Were answered sweet of days
Fair and shine,
And now I can gladly die in peace.

"Oh, My God"
I remember what I had said
Before I was born.
"wait"
That could be?
What I would ever see,
And time is not yet over with.
I had just opened my eyes
And my mind has given to me unto thought,

Much more to think about
Before I pass away,
And now I wait,
That God
Should keep his words to me.
These things shall be
At the end of days...
Those words to the day
I have seen and felt,
And now
As death awaits,
I am all is said and done.

What of this shall I see,
Of this end of all days?

104.
To Sound the Soul of Life

I hear life
In the quiet of the storm,
Naked at my birth
As to the days of dawn.
I screamed at my arrival
To sound my soul of destiny.

There is an angel
Plucking on a harp on my shoulder,
That sounds my soul
Into the songs of life.
I breathe
As I exhale the glory,
And good blessings of a beating heart,
Where there is reason enough
To sing praise.

Sitting by a giggling water fall
I hear the water trickling down the hill,
As it ripples within the many rocks
And dunks deep into the pools of blue.
Into the lake further down the way
Where a willow tree sits,
And a bird sings a daily song
In the peaceful light of early morn.

I hear the sounds of life,
Of flowers bursting buds to become life,
to seek the sky of sun

And rise above the melting snow of spring.
To glitter golden a poppy,
As the bees fly into a flowery field,
Raking honey from the nectar
Of little raped flowers,
That soon butterflies will scatter,
As they carry the pollen
To the simple things of fate.

I listen to the sun falling
As another day passes away,
And nightfall storms in
With a passion of crickets and frogs,
Singing in the brush of cat tail weeds
In a moonlight serenade.

105.
Too Sweet the Sound

Great,
The musings
Of tomorrows blessed days.
Great,
The lasting impressions
Of tomorrow's last harrah.

I shall sleep
When the night is at rest.
I will weep
In Winter's edge
And Autumn's fall.

Sweet the sound
That calls for me.
Sweet the sound
That calls for love.
That I see a snow white dove
That brings to me
The sound of love.

I am withered in Winter's age
And the leaves fall to pain.
A wind will sweep
Of the limbs that keep,
Into the wild of the willow's eyes,
To the sacred sounds of love.

Sweet the sound
That calls for love,
That the Winter shall pass
Like a fleeting dove.
As the trees shall remember
The limbs and leafs,
That once filled the grounds
To the sweet sound of love.

I fall to my knees
And cry this sound of love.
I fall like a cloud
And burst into tears of rain.
I become the beggar
Of such sweet a sound of love.
Like a bright sunlight to heat my heart,
And a dove to come bring me love.

9 781615 462315